The Art of *Biblical Conversation*

Stop Merely Reading the Bible;
Take its authors out for coffee instead!

What Readers Are Saying

Twila Higginbottom, Arkansas

There are many books written today about how to get the most out of Bible reading, and I have enjoyed many of them. Gary Collier's *The Art of Biblical Conversation* is my favorite. This little book inspires you, the reader, to 'rise up' and take your place in an engaged conversation that will challenge you and bring out your best as a child of God. It pulls back the cover to show us what is going on with our Biblical authors so that you will want to join them in this sacred Biblical conversation. It also provides 'a way' (not a method or procedure) to get the most out of your relationship with God and the sacred Word he has given us. This is a resource book that will help you discern the will of the Lord as it is revealed in our Bible then see better how to live it out in our day. I highly recommend this book.

Michael Wilkinson, M.D., F.A.C.P., Palestine, TX.

The Art of Biblical Conversation by Gary D. Collier encourages us to deeply experience our scriptures, and not just read them. In a comprehensive yet readily grasped manner, Collier explains how the authors of our scriptures were in a continual conversation with one another, even those who preceded them by centuries, and that this was done to better comprehend and converse with God. He then goes on to further explain a method that allows each of us to learn the discipline of conversing with Biblical authors, and while doing so to achieve a deeper level of intimacy with God. I highly recommend this book.

Richard Davies, Ph.D., Macon, GA

Collier points out that we use the phrase *Bible study* to cover many activities, and many of these activities don't increase our knowledge and understanding of the Bible at all. This book introduces an approach that does increase our knowledge and understanding and that is compatible with group discussion, individual study, and many other approaches to knowing the Bible. Believe me, it's worth a try.

Dennis Sutherlin, New York.

Conversation was something I was having difficulty with when discussing reading the Bible. (It just didn't seem to want to click in my brain.) This book engaged me at the start and kept me till the end. It does a great job laying this out on the table for us to see. From now on, I will stop reading and start trying to converse with the authors.

Lee Patmore, Saskatchewan, Canada

For many years now I have experienced, first-hand, Collier's dedication to a thoughtful and responsible engagement with our sacred Christian texts. Again and again what impresses me most is his commitment to a faithful reading of the text. I know of no one who holds a higher view of the Bible. But this does not mean that you will hear him parroting the standard lines; instead you will witness him blazing new trails in an effort to enrich our experience with the text. What drives Gary is his commitment to embrace the text as it stands, for what it claims to be rather than what we wish to impose upon it. And what we discover, as this book wonderfully illustrates, is that when we pay attention to how the text was born we gain the key insight in how to engage with it ourselves – in pursuit of a conversation.

Doug Lemon, Jane Lew, WV

Informative - Insightful - Instructional all describe Gary D. Collier's newest book, *The Art of Biblical Conversation.* In the footsteps of his earlier works Gary continues to produce quality material that is engaging for both the beginning Bible Student and those who have been "reading the Bible" for years.

If you can say you remember watching Black and White TV you reveal something of your age. And even if you can (as I can) remember those early days it is doubtful you would be willing to go back to the old console or table-top size entertainment device. We have become accustomed to the color version. Not just simple red, blue, green primary colors but all the subtle hues and tones, the improved clarity and definition and intensity.

The Art of Biblical Conversation will introduce you to experiencing the Bible in living color. Your Bible study will never be the same if you accept and adopt the concept of having a conversation with the authors of each of the ancient documents that are preserved in our Bible.

It is challenging -- exciting -- and worthwhile--. Pull up a chair, get a cup of coffee (or tea) and get to know Paul or Matthew or Luke (or author of your choice).

Bob Lewis,

As I have thought about *having a conversation* with biblical texts, and as I have experienced the concept while seeking to apply Gary's suggestions, it has dawned on me that I am, in a sense, "eavesdropping." By this I mean that in biblical texts we find numerous conversations between God and various people. Gary points these out. As I consider those examples, I become aware that I am "eavesdropping." Gary also talks about I-FACE as a way of checking our attitude when we read biblical texts. As an I-FACE listener, I begin to gain insights into those who are interacting within the text. I am then stimulated to ask questions of those engaged in the "conversation" within the text as if I were present with them. Near the end of the book, Gary lays out PROBE as a major guide into a conversation. Until I encountered this PROBE concept, the idea had never crossed my mind! But since my initial encounter I have been intrigued by it, and I have focused on gaining facility in the art of *Biblical Conversation.*

The ART *of* Biblical Conversation

*Stop merely reading the Bible;
take its authors out for coffee instead!*

Gary D. Collier

△ The *Dialogē* Press
ἡ διαλογή

452 W Water St., Box 121
Cloverdale, IN 46120
January 10, 2021

Publisher's Cataloging-in-Publication Data
Names: Collier, Gary D., 1950-
Title: The art of biblical conversation : stop merely reading the Bible; take its authors out for coffee instead / Gary D. Collier.
Description: Cloverdale, IN : The *Dialogē* Press, 2021. | Includes illustrations. | Summary: Defines and demonstrates the art of "biblical conversation" to deepen Bible study.
Identifiers: LCCN 20942844 | ISBN 978-0-998323091 (hardback.)
Subjects: LCSH: Bible—Study and teaching. | BISAC: RELIGION / Biblical Studies / Bible Study Guides.
Classification: LCC BS600.3.C65 S7 2020 | DDC 220.7--dc23
LC record available at https://lccn.loc.gov/2020942844

Unless otherwise indicated, all translations of Old or New Testament texts are by the author based on the following standard biblical texts: **New Testament**: *Novum Testamentum Graece*, Eberhard Nestle and Aland, Kurt (Eds.) 28th ed. (Stuttgart: Deutsche Bibelgesellschaft, 2013). **Old Testament**: *Biblia Hebraica Stuttgartensia* K. Elliger and W. Rudolph, (Eds.) (Stuttgart: Deutsche Bibelgesellschaft, 1977). Also *Septuaginta*, Alfred Rahlfs (Ed.)Deutsche Bibelgesellschaft Stuttgart, 1979

Cover art by Zoe Hagan, 2018. Used by permission.

Contact Information:
Gary D. Collier, 452 West Water St., Cloverdale, IN 46120
Phone: 765.795.3131
Email: garydcollier@CoffeewWithPaul.com
Website: http://BiblicalConversation.com

BiblicalConversation.com

For
Portia,
in honor of
Richard "RZR" Regan

Table of Contents

Figures And Tables

Appreciation

My thanks to several special people:

To *Portia Regan* for her always willing and helpful advice, consulting with me about content and design, standing by essentially on-call for days upon many late nights—this book is dedicated to her and to the memory of her husband;

To *Brian Casey* for his unflagging attention to detail amid perilous times, and for his willingness, always, to bring direct and game-changing, substantive challenges; and to Jedd for putting up with my pestering his dad so very often;

To *Twila Higginbottom* for her quiet but powerful insight and for her infinite, spirit-lifting encouragement;

Thank you all!

Thanks also to my study partners at the *Institute for the Art of Biblical Conversation (IABC)* who read this book in pre-publication status and offered feedback and comments about their experience with it. Their comments have preceded these.

Thanks also to the *IABC board of directors* for encouraging an atmosphere of open inquiry and supportive conversation about all things *biblical text*.

Most of all, and always, I am deeply touched by *Lanette's* continual attitude of openness and excitement (even still) about this book and for helping to make it possible.

Gary D. Collier
Institute for the Art of Biblical Conversation
Cloverdale, Indiana
August 2020

And the LORD used to speak to Moses
face to face,
just like one might speak with a close friend.
(Ex 33:11)

_1_

Stop Reading the Bible

For many, reading the Bible is neither easy nor enjoyable. It's a huge book, very old; it speaks in strange ways about distant places and people. There might be an interest in it, or a feeling of guilt about it ("I know I ought to read it!"), but there are many distractions.

Here's a suggestion: *Stop reading the Bible!*

I've spent years talking to Christians from all over the US about how we read the Bible individually and in groups. While most simply don't read it,[1] some spend their time in devotional booklets and call it Bible reading.

Others take part more directly in perfectly laudable Bible reading programs, such as "read the Bible in a year." This can be especially good and can offer the value of getting a hands-on big picture.

But there are drawbacks, even here. For one thing, the object of the year-long program is to read through the books (i.e., to get *through* them), not engage them on any kind of deep level. Furthermore, reading is too often from unexamined and

---

[1] Studies confirm this (e.g., Barna in Collier 2012, 54f). (See bibliography for titles)

entrenched perspectives that never get challenged and that get in the way of the texts themselves. Sometimes, we can't see the biblical forest for our own particular trees.

Intimacy

The appeal made in this book is simple:

> *Stop merely reading the Bible!*
> *Romance it! Dance with it!*
> *Aspire to deep-level conversation!*

The imagery is purposely the language of romance. Intimacy is the goal.

This is no novel way of speaking. The biblical book, *Song of Songs,* sings about intimate relations between a man and woman. That is clearly the main topic. But throughout history the understanding of this book is filled with allegorical depictions of *divine* love (e.g., God and Israel, Christ and the Church, God and the individual). Indeed, a few texts within the song help to fire such imaginative applications:

BELOVED:
Set me like a seal on your heart,
like a seal on your arm.
For love is strong as Death,
passion as relentless as Sheol.
The flash of it is a flash of fire,
a flame of Yahweh himself!
(Song of Songs 8:6 NJB)

Divine love. It would be interesting to explore this song as an allegory between a reader and beloved sacred texts.[2]

Even Psalm 119:97 can be translated with terms of intimacy from both Hebrew and Greek,

---

[2] I'm not suggesting that such an allegorical reading would have been the *intention* of the author(s) of this song, as if any such intention could actually be established for this particular song. This song comes to us without context and it would be impossible to affix with any certainty a specific original intention. I'm merely suggesting a potential allegorical relevancy.

Oh how I love your law,
it is the object of my *affection* all day long!

Or another way, still:

it is my ongoing *conversation* all day long!

As with a lover, "I talk about her/him all day long!"

A much later example gets even more specific by depicting the Torah[3] as a bride on her wedding night. In 13th century Spain, a Jewish mystical text (with the intriguing title, *The Book of Splendor*) spoke out against a tendency in some Jewish circles to sift the Torah philosophically, stripping it of it's mystery to satisfy "logical" reading agendas.

> Rabbi Simeon said: If a man looks upon the Torah as merely a book presenting narratives and everyday matters, alas for him!. . . The Torah, in all of its worlds, holds supernal truths and sublime secrets. . .

The text continues that, for the sake of humanity, the Torah had

> garbed herself in garments of this world. The tales related in the Torah are simply her outer garments, and woe to the man who regards that outer garb as the Torah itself, for such a man will be deprived of portion . . . what is underneath. . . . Woe to sinners who look upon the Torah as simply tales pertaining to things of the world, seeing thus only the outer garment.[4]

It is not my intent to extend this analogy, but I do wish to focus on the notion of intimacy when reading a sacred text, that it should not be held at a distance in order to *get through* it. One should rather slow down; romance a sacred text; dance with it; have an intimate conversation.

Deep-level conversation is the goal—not a cavalier reading; not idle chit-chat about it. Two iconic texts will serve to illustrate this.

---

[3] The Jewish Bible. Can also refer to the Pentateuch, depending on context.
[4] As quoted in Fishbane 1989, 34. (See bibliography for titles.)

Jesus and Company

In the first story, Jesus and three disciples walk up a mountain (Lk 9:29-31).

> *And it happened while he was praying that the appearance of his face became different and his garment became as white as lightning; and all of a sudden, two men were engaged in a conversation with him: none other than Moses and Elijah! The three of them were standing there in radiant splendor and they were discussing the exodus of Jesus, which was about to be fulfilled in Jerusalem.*[5]

This is quite a story! Moses and Elijah strike up a conversation with Jesus over what's about to happen in Jerusalem. This encounter presumably began late into the night or very early morning after Peter, James, and John had fallen into a *heavy sleep*[6] while Jesus was praying—they would not have been aware of the beginning of the event! They are then jolted awake as they catch a glimpse of Jesus shimmering with *glory* as he kept on talking with these two titans from the past. And as this astounding meeting is winding down, Peter, apparently disoriented, blurts out some nonsense.[7]

---

[5] Unless otherwise noted, all translations from Greek or Hebrew texts are my own. See copyright page for texts used.

[6] *Heavy sleep* implies that the encounter went on for at least some time. In Luke, the phrase does not mean "almost asleep" or "falling asleep"; this is heavy sleep. If we compare similar phrases in a different story, Mt 26:43; Mk 14:40; and also Philo *Ebr.* 131, they all show that the phrase in Luke implies being asleep. See BDAG and Friberg for details. The latter says: "literally be burdened by sleep, i.e. be sound asleep (Lk 9.32)." Friberg also compares this with Acts 20:9 καταφέρεσθαι ὕπνῳ (*kataferesthai hupnō*) and says "literally be carried away by sleep, i.e. become more and more sleepy." Most people can identify with this, the kind of sleep that weighs one down into heavy bouts of it; a tugging sleep where one cannot hold the eyes open despite efforts to do so (like a mom staying up all night with a sick child, careworn from worry; or a driver struggling to stay awake at the wheel; or a student attempting to finish a paper before a deadline; even possibly dreaming during these short intervals, and also possibly being jolted awake with a little or a lot of disorientation).

[7] By Luke's wording, we can see them groggily waking up from a deep sleep only to catch sight of this incredible event, and this jolted them awake. Luke tells this story differently from the other Gospels, focusing on the *glory* of Jesus with the other two—an utterly astounding sight! By doing this, Peter is shown as befuddled by what he woke up to and as making no sense in his comments. Notice the following details: (1) Only Luke has vv. 31-33a, and this moves *glory* (13x in Lk) into the main spot in this story (see especially 9:26). (2) This explains Peter's rather abrupt (and off-base) pronouncement about wanting to build some shrines—he does not know what he is saying because he (and his friends) were disoriented by the sight they woke up to. (3) This is

Now, usually, when reading this or any Gospel story, we are taught to run over to the other Gospels and *mash them together*[8] with this one, so that they all end up telling the same story. But *a conversation* with any text asks you *not* to do that. Dance with Luke's text for awhile. Look at the story this author is telling and the way he is telling it. There is nothing wrong with eventually comparing the various stories; but there is also everything right with paying attention to one writer at a time.[9]

English translations of Luke's story are not always as vivid or picturesque as the paraphrase above. Older translations were quite matter-of-fact. We are told that Jesus "talked" with them and that they "spoke" with him.

KJV/ASV[10] =	talked...	spake
RSV/NIRV/DBY/ WEB =	talked...	spoke
NIV/CSB/ESV/CEB =	talking...	spoke

One could almost get the impression from these translations that this was only a momentary thing. These are not incorrect translations, they're just flat. The Greek text is more nuanced than this, and some newer translations begin to show this.

NET =	began talking...	spoke
NAB/MIT =	were conversing...	spoke
YLT =	were speaking...	spoke

Other translations get even more specific.

NRS/NJB/NAS /CSB17=	were talking...	were speaking
MIT/ROT=	were conversing...	were speaking

Technically, both of these verbs are stated in a way to subtly imply that the talking lasted awhile. The newer translations are helpful, here, because they bring out what the Greek text is

---

not so in Mark, where the point is *fear*, not glory (only 3x in Mk, and is not in this story). (4) It is also not so in Matthew where *glory* (7x in Mt) is not at all associated with this story; instead, this story is tied up with the larger Peter-story being told throughout Matthew.

[8] I mean by this too quickly combining the 4 stories into one. See previous note.

[9] After all, Luke says specifically that he's trying to be a bit different from others about Jesus. Lk 1:1-2. Sometimes Christian readers assume that Luke is not including Matthew and Mark in this statement. That is an unwarranted assumption.

[10] For English translation abbreviations see Appendix.

implying—that Jesus was engaged in a *conversation* that went on for some time with Moses and Elijah.

Just thinking about this in the context of Luke's whole Gospel fires the imagination. Here, Moses (the giver of the Law) and Elijah (at the head of the Prophets) are standing with the anointed one (Lk 4:18)—the one about whom they had written—and they were having *a prolonged, focused conversation* over what God was about to do in the world.

The story is not saying "the OT is no good any more—only Jesus!" Quite the contrary, it is showing disciples of Jesus how to understand sacred texts in light of Jesus. In Luke, this sets the stage for several things, including Lk 24:44 where Jesus explains *the Law, the Prophets, and the Psalms* to his disciples and shows them how to read those sacred texts through the new light of Jesus' teachings. Earlier (Lk 5:37) the Pharisees did not get it, so Jesus compares them to old wineskins about to burst.

Clearly, in Luke, the story is about Jesus in glory at this moment, a concept that shows up three times in this one chapter (9:26, 31, 32).[11] But among other things, this story can be understood as a heads-up to Jesus-followers about how to envision sacred texts. It is not about three guys who are shooting the breeze on a mountain top; it is a story that represents *conversations among sacred texts—how some texts interact with others.* It represents that *conversations with previously written texts* are not only common but ongoing. Biblical authors have these conversations among themselves all the time about what God has done, is now doing, and is about to do.

This is more than a nice thought, it is a stunning picture of how our sacred texts came into existence—in literal interaction with one another. For example, later in Luke (19:46), Jesus says,

---

[11] The noun and verb "glory, to glorify," occurs 22 times in Luke, but only 4 times in Mark and 11 times in Matthew. Only John (which does not tell this story) has more, with 61. The story in Luke is connected to glory.

"My house will be called a house of prayer"
  (Isa 56:7),
"but you have made it into a den of insurrectionists!"
  (Jer 7:11)

In this text,

1. Jesus again sets Isaiah in conversation with Jeremiah,

2. who was already in conversation with 1Sam 4:10f.

3. Now Jesus enters that conversation and draws his followers in as well.

This is quite a conversation! And this is not unusual in biblical texts. Unfortunately (far too often), we have *not been trained* to see these things, and just maybe *we have been trained* not to see them.

In summary, this the first story (Jesus and Company) offers a glimpse. It is a vivid model for (1) how biblical authors converse among themselves to speak of God at work in the world, and (2) how disciples of Jesus are to wake up to those intimate conversations; i.e., wake up as listeners, not as talkers!

Jacob and the Wrestler

The second is a prolonged and intriguing story from Genesis 32—I'll quote only 32:24, 26.

> *So Jacob was left, now, by himself. And a man wrestled with him all night until morning. . . . Then the man said: "Let me get up, for the sun is coming up!" But Jacob said, "I won't let you go till you bless me!"* [12]

A man struggling with God? Or God interacting with mankind? These are the questions of these early texts. And we are still asking them! If we stay with the text for awhile—dance with it—we see that the struggle takes place on multiple levels. One is *the struggle of those who would read such texts. The text is calling out for more*

---

[12] This is a translation of the Greek OT (LXX) text, which is 32:25-27.

than a mere speed-read; it is modeling for us not to let go without a blessing. What an old, old, old—delightful—story.

But let's go back, as we should, and dance with this text some more. Jacob is all by himself near the Jabbok river when, without warning, the text says very matter-of-factly: "a man was wrestling with him until the early morning." Every time I read this story, I look two or three times to see if I've missed the introduction of this man. I do this double-take because I feel like Eddie Murphy in "Trading Places" when he, as a homeless man being offered a million dollar home and a butler of his own, says sarcastically, "This happens to me every week!" Well, of course, it doesn't. This story about Jacob is strange; as Jacob was in the dark, so are we. (That is a design of the story.)

By the end of the story, if we grapple with it, it starts becoming clear. Jacob goes through a personal (intimate) experience of struggle that forever changes him, just prior to a major "turning point event" in his life (in this case, his being reunited with his brother Esau, whom he had cheated out of his birthright years before). Jacob emerges broken by God, but then he is re-named and redirected with God's blessing. A powerful, powerful story.

Like two men wrestling, this story has several overlapping layers: (1) like *wrestling* being written in a form that implies in both Hebrew and Greek[13] an *ongoing, rolling* struggle (just like "conversing" and "speaking" in the Jesus-story above). Here the struggle went on for a good long time. (2) In Hebrew there is a wordplay between "wrestle" (*yēobēq*), the river "Jabbok" (*yabboq*), and the name Jacob (*ya'ăqob* "one who contends"). (3) Jacob gets his name changed to Israel ("one who contends with God"), which erases his shoddy past as one who from birth continually cheated others. (4) He leaves with a limp, meaning this was no mere vision for him, but also that struggles with God have many kinds of outcomes. (5) Only then do we find out that the man in v. 26 is God in human form (vv. 28, 30), so that Jacob ends up blurting

---

[13] Called the *imperfect tense* in both languages, these are not identical, and there is more involved than this; but both Hebrew and Greek can be fairly translated (because of context) that "he was wrestling with him up to the point of early morning."

out in amazement: "I saw God face to face, *and yet I survived!*" (v. 30). This is a turning point for him—a drastic change in direction.

It is at the heart of this story, as they were wrestling toward morning, that the man (in a leg-lock?) asks to be released. And Jacob says with great emphasis: *"I won't let you go unless you bless me!"* This cries out for multiple applications; it begs for readers and hearers to grapple with the story until blessed. This is God reaching out to humankind to understand the importance of every struggle.

Like the story of Jesus on the mountain before a significant event, this one, too, is rich with deeper possibilities, specifically now for *how we ourselves might not just read, but grapple with biblical texts—dance with them!*—that in reading, we strive to understand, sometimes even into the wee hours of the morning, holding on dearly to our Bibles with the resolve that: "I will not let you go till you bless me!"

A Visit to My Home

> Oh, for the days when I was in my prime,
> when God's *intimate friendship* blessed my house!

That's Job 29:4 in the NIV. But in the Greek OT version, the second line is provocative:

> *when God would pay visits to my home!*

What a picture this paints!

Whether romantic language is used or not, *intimacy with God* is our goal. Like the two stories in this first chapter (1) Jesus with Moses and Elijah, and (2) Jacob wrestling with God, we need to break out of simplistic reading habits. These two stories will help structure the rest of this book.

Part 1: Opportunity is a big-picture introduction designed to lift up our Bible-reading vision. These five chapters will collectively point out *that Christians too often take Bible reading as a purely personal act, where "I'm free to pick the style of reading*

I like best." Such an approach takes a book that is the product of the best thinking of numerous generations of people and turns it into the great, ego-stroking, self-help book from the sky. Part 1 will utterly reject this by clarifying the opportunity in front of us; namely, that we embrace various thoughtful styles of reading for how they interact—a kind of orchestra of intimate conversation with biblical authors through their texts.

Part 2: Journey is the heart and soul of this book. Without it, the book will fall apart as merely "cool things we might try." It is here that the model of Jesus with Moses and Elijah comes front and center. Here we will journey firsthand into *how biblical authors interact in conversation with each other*—as though they are literally talking to one another about what it means to be in pursuit of God. We will distinguish three shades of conversation, and we will look specifically at one major example: the apostle Paul in conversation with Jewish authors and traditions before him. Not a "Sunday school" discussion, this will challenge you! You need to sit up straight, open your Bible, and engage in the process. If you don't, it is possible you will simply "not get it."

The reason Part 2 might be challenging for some is not because it is too technical or academic;[14] it will be because this notion of *Biblical Conversation* will seem so totally new to many readers. But it is *not* new; it is in fact as old as the biblical texts themselves.

PART 3: TRANSFORMATION of your Bible-reading life— that's what this is about! Nothing short of a Bible-reading revolution. That becomes the specific goal. If you see this is just another book to read—one that you can finish, agree or disagree with, and then set aside and ignore, then nothing is going to happen; nothing at all will change.

But these chapters want more from you. They don't just say, "We need to do a better job reading the Bible!" No, they reach out to you and challenge you to do something bold and new. Here we embrace the model of Jacob wrestling with God. It is here that *we ourselves* are being invited to engage in (to become part of) that

---

[14] Some will use that as a way out.

ongoing intertextual, inner-biblical,[15] intimate, conversation (that we will see in Part 2)—not letting go till we are blessed. The goal, here, is very clear: that we go beyond *merely* reading the Bible!

But first, if God is going to pay a visit to my home, I have to get beyond the problem of jargon. I have to see with new eyes what the opportunity actually is. If I can't do that, I'm stuck in a rut.

---

[15] The technical terms *intertextual* and *inner-biblical* both refer to the intricate ways that biblical authors interact or interpret each other. This is also described as texts interacting with other texts. For a technical definition of the former, see Collier 2020, 603; and then 286-94 for a full discussion.

PART 1: OPPORTUNITY

Too often, Bible readers are like the Corinthians:
"I follow Paul, or Apollos, or Cephas, or Christ!"
*We don't see the **opportunity** in front of us.*
We adopt a single style of reading,
and we act as if it is the one and only true way:
"I like devotional reading, or deep textual study,
or reading for the sake of history,
or Spirit-led reading!"

But dancing with biblical texts cannot be
so vacuous or narrow minded;
it requires a wide variety of well-thought-out styles.

We begin with a big-picture look at
the problem of Jargon,
followed by the interplay of Spirit, Text, and Self.

2

Beyond Jargon

"A conversation with biblical authors": The problem with this short phrase is that hardly anyone associates the word *conversation* with reading the Bible. With Prayer? Definitely! Prayer is often called "a conversation with God." More than occasionally someone will remark, "Oh, I've had conversations with God all my life!" But to speak the phrase "a conversation with biblical authors"—one might as well be speaking in a foreign language.

Some will respond with honest confusion: "I'm not sure what this means! I have difficulty seeing how Bible reading can rightly be called a *conversation!*" Others might display less patience, like the man who said to me rather abruptly and with more than a little frustration: "It's not *actually* a conversation, is it! *Reading* is simply *reading!*" I replied to him: "If 'simply reading' is all you want, then that is all you will ever get." This was not a dismissal; it was an invitation to allow for the possibility of something more.

What needs to be seen is that the word *conversation* is rarely used by anyone for interactions with biblical texts. Among Christians, *reading* is one thing; *conversation* is another. There is a built-in, conceptual gulf between them.

So why bother? Why use the term at all? The answer is simple: *Because conversation is what is actually happening! Biblical authors are conversing with each other, and they are inviting us to join the conversation.* The fact that Christians have a long tradition of closing their eyes to that invitation is no reason to keep doing it.

The problem is, there's a lot of jargon floating around in Christian circles that keep us out of the conversation.

Popular Jargon

We are more likely to hear words like *daily reading,* or *devotional reading,* or *reading through a year,* or *reading schedule,* or more heady words like *context,* or *historical background,* or even *the Hebrew or Greek says,* and on like that. Or maybe we'll hear words like "It's a big book!" or "Some of it is hard to understand!" or "I know I should," or "no time." All of these are genuine statements by people feeling a need, desire, or warmth about reading the Bible. But hardly anybody speaks about it as a *conversation.*

Another word also belongs in this list: *prophecy.* It is often thought of as its own subject and often talked about in stark, unidirectional, polar terms—like this:

Pole 1   Pole 2
Prophecy ━━━━━━━━━━━━━━━━▶ Fulfilment

But this is like describing the universe as a 2-dimensional pencil sketch with a few planets and stars. Far better is to depict prophecy in "3-D" conversational terms, where authors and texts are intersecting, overlapping, and interacting with others, just like conversations traverse and crisscross one another—not in a nice, neat, straight line, but as an ever-growing dialog over time among Jewish and Christian texts.

Biblical prophecy is an incredible and fascinating study of textual interrelation, where authors continually are calling up previous texts and ideas, and they are ever-exploring possible new applications of those ideas in new situations.

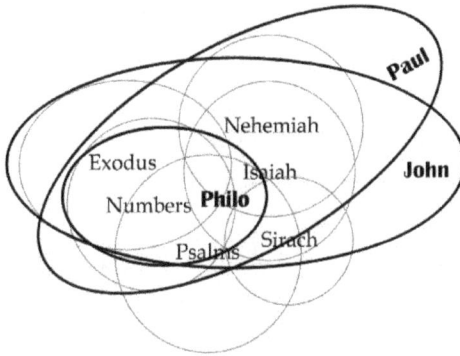

Figure 1: 3D Conversation

Far too often in American Christianity, prophecy is viewed for its *current apologetic* value more than for the interactive nature and function of prophecy in its ancient near eastern biblical contexts. As a result, *prophecy* is often associated with "lists of prophecies" that are then said to "prove the Bible," even though no biblical prophecy ever presents itself as proving a book or a particular canon (i.e., a list) of books. So, there has developed a long-standing interest in tallying up the numbers of prophecies in the OT and NT as a way of constituting proof that the Bible is inspired.

There are numerous books and internet pages, for example, that specifically claim to "prove the Bible" with such lists. So Payne 1980 (J. Barton Payne, *Encyclopedia of Biblical Prophecy: The Complete Guide to Scriptural Predictions and Their Fulfillment*) is often cited for listing 1,239 prophecies OT; 578 prophecies NT, for a grand total of 1,817—over a total of 8,352 verses in the Bible. It is then claimed by those who use Payne's resource for this purpose, that nearly one fourth of the Bible is prophecy fulfilled, thus overwhelmingly proving that the Bible is "true."

In such a "counting prophecies" approach, the focus is not *descriptive* (how prophecies actually work in specific texts), but *constitutive* (how we can use the numbers to prove our own

31

interest). In such a practice, prophecy is domesticated—like a lap dog—for our own purposes.

It would be especially valuable to ask two questions about biblical prophecy: (1) "How was inter-biblical *conversation* between biblical authors affecting and shaping prophecy, and causing it to actually function?" (i.e., Jesus, Moses, Elijah); and (2) "How can we become part of that *conversation* even today?" (i.e., Jacob wrestling with God).

By exploring these two questions, we just might begin to see how biblical texts actually work *in conversation* with each other; and we also might rediscover how to *engage in that ancient conversation* ourselves.

But the word *conversation* is not used by any one for these things.

Academic Jargon

Biblical scholars of all shapes and sizes have a long history of talking about reading the Bible. There are many books on method and process, on skill development and practice. The efforts to help people read the Bible for all it's worth and not cage it like a blue parakeet flow from intense faith and integrity of practice.[16]

Scholars also talk a lot about biblical prophecy—more specifically they speak about the relation of the OT and NT. They tend not to speak in the "counting prophesies" language; they tend, instead, to focus on the mechanics of how texts intersect and interact, and they use strange phrases like the following:

- *New Testament use of the Old Testament*
- *inner biblical exegesis*
- *midrash* or *comparative midrash*
- *intertextuality*
- *typology*
- *figural interpretation*

---

[16] An allusion, here, to only three books: Fay 2013, Fee 2014; and McKnight 2008 (see bibliography for titles). But these are only three of an incredibly long list of books.

- *reading backwards*
- *reading backwards and forwards*

The word *conversation* is not on this list.

In 2014 Richard Hays published the now highly popular *Reading Backwards*; followed in 2016 by *Echoes of Scripture in the Gospels*. In 2017, Ben Witherington wanted to talk about reading both backwards and forwards. All of these terms are how the topic of OT and NT are talked about. But *conversation* is not a word used for this.

Not too long ago I stood in line at an academic conference, and a young man next to me (from a well-known academic institution) was introducing himself. He saw my name tag with *"Institute for the Art of Biblical Conversation (IABC),"* and he half mumbled, "I don't know what that means." It is not the language his teachers or the books he was reading were using.

So the point is clear: up till now, the word *conversation* is not a word anybody uses for reading biblical texts. For prayer? Yes! But not for how biblical authors interact with each other, and not for asking how we might become part of that interaction.

Beyond Jargon

One practice has long puzzled me: when *we* do the talking and believe God speaks back to us during prayer, we call it conversation; but when *God* does the talking from what we call "the very words of God" (the Bible), we merely call that *reading*. Maybe this is because, in *reading*, we can stay safely on the outside looking in with no meaningful part in the process. It's not thought to be as *up close and personal* as prayer.

This should not be that surprising; it reflects actual, developed, argued views of the Bible. "It" is truly outside of us, apart from us, and aimed at us. "It" is written for us and to us, certainly not by us. "It" is so *completely of God*, there is no part that could possibly be *of us*. So just maybe we've decided that *the God of the Bible* doesn't always sound as warm, friendly, and understanding as *the*

33

God of our prayers. So when *we* do the talking and feel in our hearts that God is speaking back, it's a conversation; but when *God* does the talking (in what we somewhat ironically call "His Word"), *we* now see ourselves as recipients, not participants.

Maybe there's a better way to think about prayer and Bible reading. *Maybe both are conversations—just different aspects and levels of it.*

To get beyond current jargon and become comfortable with the word *conversation* we must realize that it implies participation, and that has not yet been incorporated into our language about reading the Bible. It needs to happen.

Way back in 2004, when "Coffee With Paul" (now IABC) was founded, a few of us began talking about *Biblical Conversation* as a more descriptive way of presenting what is happening (1) within and among biblical texts, and (2) what should happen with us as we interact with those texts and authors. Several books explore this landscape:[17]

1. In 1993, *The Forgotten Treasure: Reading the Bible Like Jesus* actually predates and helped lay the groundwork for a *conversation* with Matthew over coffee.

2. In 2012, *Scripture, Canon, & Inspiration* took our first steps in specifically exploring the roots of biblical texts, as well as the nature of canon and inspiration, describing them all as "an act of faith, by people of faith, in search of a *conversation* with God."

3. In 2017 (and updated in 2018, 2019, and 2020), *I Paulos* offered a full, studied critique (4 volumes, 740 total pages) of standard approaches to the Bible while also presenting a detailed, in-depth case for *Biblical Conversation* by way of one letter of Paul: 1Thessalonians.

4. In 2018, the book *Graphē in Biblical and Related Literature* focused on a single important word in biblical texts to

---

[17] The reason for listing these books, or for talking about *IABC* at any point in this book, is merely to show that we have given a great deal of thought to this. This is not a passing interest.

demonstrate how to have a *conversation* with just one word: the word normally translated as *scripture* in all current translations.

5. In 2019, a new and innovative book, *Scribes Trained for the Kingdom,* provided a pre-grammar for approaching NT Greek as a means of spiritual *conversation.*

After all of this time and effort, one thing is clear: this topic is not at all a matter of semantics—"you say *tomayto, and I say tomahto."*

The question before us is straightforward: how can we best visualize and then imaginatively describe what is actually going on (1) within and between *biblical texts and authors* (as with Jesus, Moses, and Elijah); and (2) among *us* as we attempt to become part of a conversation with them (like Jacob wrestling with God)?

Are we supposed to be merely readers? Are we simply outsiders looking in?

Or are we to be *engaged, energetic—even imaginative—participants* in one of the most impressive and longest-running conversations the world has ever seen?

Styles of Reading

Not only does Jargon sometimes stand in the way, how people choose to read the Bible is just as big a problem.

Way too many Christians approach Bible reading "by default"— i.e., they choose whatever style of reading that makes them feel most comfortable:

"I like devotional reading!"
"I like deep textual study!"
"I like to read for history/facts."
"I just read by the Spirit of God!"

As simple statements, there is nothing wrong with any of these. But when they exist outside the context of a careful reading approach, they simply become excuses to do whatever one wants with biblical texts. By themselves, they are not only poor and insufficient reading strategies, they do not provide any ability to engage biblical authors in any kind of deep-level conversation.

It is helpful to note that the above list represents four general, overarching styles of reading.[18] A graph will illustrate. This is an oversimplification of the reading spectrum merely to depict that anyone who reads attending to only one area will be a lopsided reader.

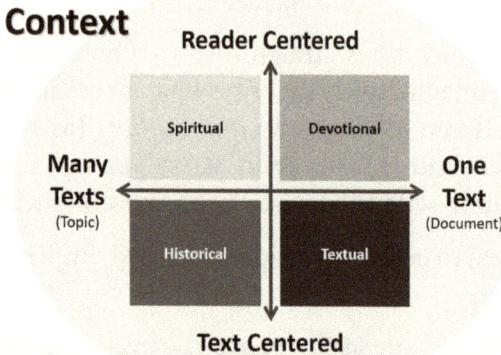

Figure 2: Reading Grid

So then, in the next three chapters, we will talk about reading for Spirit, Text, and Self, since these are often treated as isolated reading styles or approaches; namely, when anyone says, "This is how I read!" We will show how all of these relate to each other and how they need each other for an integrated, healthy conversational approach to biblical authors through their texts.

---

[18] Naturally, the "reading spectrum" could be listed in far more detail. For a 25-minute explanatory video using a chart similar to this, see the second video on the page https://coffeewithpaul.com/probe/.

_3_

Spirit

All reading of biblical texts
should be Spirit-led.
All!

Most people agree with this, at least in theory. The question is
how to apply it. Does it mean we don't need to learn or follow
methods or rules of interpretation? Some say yes to this: who
needs dried-up old "methods" when you have the ever-new Spirit
of God? It sounds good, but it lacks basic understanding. In effect,
it turns *reading by the spirit* into a super-method—the method
beyond all others, rendering the rest superfluous.

So, let's complete, now, the opening line.

*Spirit-led Bible reading is not a **method**;*
it is an attitude of submission to God's Spirit
on the part of the reader
no matter what methods or rules
one follows when reading—
whether mere reflection, meditation,
or some form of focused textual study.

Acceptance of the above two pronouncements will solve all
kinds of misconceptions that show up in this so-called debate.
Honestly, who in their right mind would seriously advocate any

approach to Bible reading that is *not* Spirit-led? Would any follower of Jesus ever say, "I want the Spirit of God to stay away when I read the Bible?" This would be nonsense.

The Letter Kills?

Everybody knows that law is made for people, not people for law. Law for its own sake kills—so also with rules and methods. Everybody knows: the letter kills.

But everybody also knows what happens when there are no laws, no rules, and no methods or procedures.

Let's ask Paul in 2Cor 3:6—the same Paul who said "I think I have the Spirit of God": [19]

"Hey, Paul, how do *you* read the scriptures?"

If we pay attention, he will answer us:

God has made us competent as ministers of a new covenant—not of the letter but of the Spirit;
for *the letter kills, but the Spirit gives life.* (NIV)

Now this is sometimes used as a kind of champion text against study rules or methods because *the Spirit leads* and *the letter kills.* But what is so interesting is how such an approach virtually ignores the context of 2Corinthians 3—as if the Spirit of God is giving them a private "pass" by saying: "It doesn't matter what that old dead text says; I, the living Spirit, am speaking into your heart what you really need to know!"

Perhaps it would be a good idea to note that 2Corinthians 3 shows us how Paul is overtly reading Exodus 34—which means that, here, Paul gives a specific example of how he reads a biblical text. So we can watch how Paul explicitly engages Exodus 34 in an intricate, method-based conversation to make his argument for his own readers. To say this a bit more technically, if we look closely, we can actually watch Paul read Exodus 34 midrashically.

---

[19] 1Cor 7:40

Now, midrash[20] means that he is utilizing ancient Jewish methods of interpretation that are similar to later rabbis. He certainly does not brag about, or spell out, require, or even mention the methods he uses—he never does that. But he clearly does use accepted methods and approaches[21] (not only here in this text, but in other places as well[22]). So he is absolutely not saying "I don't follow rules and methods, I just read by the Spirit!"

As mentioned above, this is the same Paul who said: "I think I have the Spirit of God."

The bottom line is that Paul is *not* claiming (in this text or any other) that Spirit-led reading is a "method" that somehow renders all other methods of reading obsolete. That would be just plain silly! Can you imagine someone asking Paul: "What do you think of the Spirit-led method of Bible reading?" To make statements that study methods are somehow opposed to "reading by the Spirit" is to misunderstand Paul completely.

All readings of biblical texts should be Spirit-led.
And if any method of reading is Spirit-led,
it will at least attempt to be responsible to
what that text is trying to say and do.

This should be emphasized:

The Spirit of God
will never lead anyone away from
the Word of God.

---

[20] This is a key term in later chapters. To give a technical description: *midrash* is an ancient, pre-scientific, non-western term, based wholly in now distant philosophical systems and worldviews. The word was clearly developing in its usage, from the basic to a more complex and varied. It is a mistake to try to arrive at a single meaning of *midrash* that can be applied to all periods of time or situations. For my part, I have offered great detail in Collier 2020, 261-85, that the term מדרש|*midrash* in its earliest usage in biblical texts (1) was associated with the telling and/or retelling of a distinctively Jewish story: a YHWH Story; and (2) was concerned with how that YHWH story functioned as an ongoing "deliverance" story. That is to say, it is best described, in its early uses, as *telling the YHWH story now!* **It is not** "How can this old text *be applied* now?" **It is instead** "How is this sacred text *speaking* now?

[21] Any current major commentary on 2Corinthians 3 will lay this out.

[22] E.g., 1Cor 10:1-11; Rom 10:5-13; Eph 4:8 and more.

Lessons Learned

Let's see if we can draw out a couple of lessons from this:

First, to read by the Spirit of God does not mean that you need to be a biblical scholar or that Bible reading has to be complicated. As a matter of plain fact, to enjoy and be touched by the many stories found in the Bible, you need no special knowledge about history, religion, or politics; no particular kind of education or social status; and no amount of money. Biblical stories have universal appeal: stories about women and men, prophets and kings, nations and gods, peacetime and war, life and death—indeed, about all aspects of human existence. Anyone can read the Bible and benefit from it—even children!

Second, to read by the Spirit of God does not mean that you are now free to ignore sound study methods and principles, as if they don't even matter.

It may be that on some levels, stories in the Bible can be read and appreciated even by children. But the Bible is not a children's book! It is a big and diverse book, and there are many complicated things in it that require the very best thinking adults can bring to it.

And yet, it is amazing how quickly some people can slip (or jump headlong!) into a childish mode of Spirit-talk as a kind of end-run around all of the complications. There is a particular kind of defiant insistence among some people that since they don't need to be a scholar to read the Bible, then they don't want to hear about a bunch of complicated "methods" or "rules" of interpretation. Why care at all about Hebrew or Greek texts, or English translations, or any other such scholar-laden thing? After all, Christians live by the Spirit of God, not the letter of any law, rules, or methods—right? Surely the Spirit of God can guide Christ followers to every full extent!

Right?

It sounds good—the Spirit rescuing us from the folly of rules and such. Who will say that the Spirit can't grant our three wishes?

"I just read my Bible, and the Spirit tells me all I need to know. Who needs rules when you've got the Spirit!"

Well *of course* if we rely on law for its own sake we go too far. If we think rules and methods are the true ticket into heaven, or must be forced on anyone at all, then we go too far! But why would any follower of Jesus, after a time of initiation into first things, not want to know more about how to read "God's book" better and more responsibly? Any mentality that sets the Spirit of God into an antinomian context (i.e. a lawless context, one that is "anti-rules") did not get that from the Spirit, and indeed does not understand the Spirit of God! When we grow up, and are no longer children, we need to learn how to think like adults:

*All reading of biblical texts
should be Spirit-led.*
ALL!

*Spirit-led Bible reading is not a **method**;
it is an attitude of submission to God's Spirit
on the part of the reader
no matter what methods or rules
one follows when reading—
whether mere reflection, meditation,
or some form of focused textual study.*

Beyond Schizophrenia

Think about this. You don't have to be a scholar to read the Bible. You also don't have to be a medical doctor.

But when your 12 year old daughter needs a kidney transplant, would you turn her over for medical treatment to a good Christian who is strong in the Spirit of God, but who never went to medical school even one day?

No?

Don't you believe in the Spirit? Are you trying to make this complicated? Just read the Bible!

These signs will accompany those who believe: In my name . . . **they will place their hands on the sick and they will be well.**" (Mk. 16:17 NET)

and to another gifts of **healing by the one Spirit**, (1Cor 12:9; see also Lk 9:42; Acts 10:38).

Tell me I'm wrong about this. If you allow the Spirit to guide you about your daughter who needs a kidney transplant, the Spirit of God will NOT tell you to boycott all doctors. The Spirit will instead tell you to *find medically trained people who know what they are doing to help your daughter—and that would also **include** some people who are strong in the Spirit of God*. The fact is, the texts quoted above were not written to turn you into an idiot so that you can harm your children "in the name of God!"

So how about we dump our spiritual schizophrenia and use the intelligence God gave us when reading the Bible.

Let's be clear about this.

First, the Spirit of God can work through anybody at any time— even through biblical scholars; and yes, even through those rules and methods of biblical interpretation. For all we know, the Spirit of God is the one who *revealed* these methods to all those scholars. Reading the Bible by the Spirit of God is an attitude, not a method, and it is not a replacement for sound methods.

So while you may not want to become a scholar yourself (which is just fine), that does not mean that you have freedom to do with texts whatever you feel like doing while blaming your decisions on the Holy Spirit of God. Nor does it mean that scholars are of no value to you and that you should be arrogant towards them (nor they towards you) as if you have nothing to learn from them.

Second, being led by the Spirit when reading the Bible does NOT mean that the Spirit will do all of your work for you. The Spirit of God is not an excuse for you to be lazy! If the Spirit really is leading you in Bible reading, you will drop any notion that the Spirit has somehow made you some kind of ridiculous promise that it will always whisper in your ear the answer to every question you decide to ask. That's the genie in the bottle, not the Holy Spirit of God.

This needs to be clearly understood: *Spirit-led Bible reading is not a method; it is an attitude of submission to God's Spirit on the part of the reader no matter what methods or rules one follows when reading, whether mere reflection, deep meditation, or textual study.*[23]

Submit to the Spirit of God! When we do that in deed and not word only, we find ourselves *wanting* to know more about sound methods that help us engage in true conversation with some of the most precious texts ever written in the world.

---

[23] I would like to thank Dr. Mike Parker, a former professor of pathology for 30 years at the University of Oklahoma College of Medicine, a long-time church leader, and a personal friend. At his initiation, we carried on an extended email discussion about the topic of the role of the Spirit in Bible reading that consisted of 12 lengthy emails from September 27 to October 2, 2019. That discussion (like iron with iron) helped me to think through my wording for this chapter.

4

Text

It is not in spite of, but because of our love for our ancient, precious biblical texts, that we, with energy, seek out how to read them. We respect *methods* developed over centuries, and they are not the painful things that some imagine or accuse them of being; they are blessings from God that make it possible for us to dance with our texts in a wide variety of styles to help make intimate conversation possible.

Methods are different from tools. *Tools* for Bible reading include things like English translations, concordances, dictionaries, Greek and Hebrew texts, commentaries, Bible software, and the like. *Methods,* on the other hand, are the dance steps we learn to allow conversation with biblical texts to come alive—a conversation between the *text* and the *self*.[24]

Methods are so important for reading biblical texts that we'll spend two chapters on this sketching out an array of methods under two major categories:

---

[24] I will speak of "the *self*" or "our *self*" as used in psychology. See Baker 2020.

1	2
Methods for the Text: Used for textual and contextual evaluation and study	***Methods for the Self:*** Used for personal introspection and contemplation

As we proceed, I will point out that these two categories are not entirely separate; for either to work properly they must work together. They are, in effect, joined at the hip.

However, I want to first deal with an objection. Have I forced the parallelism? Does the word "methods" apply more to #1 than #2? Are they apples and oranges?

I include this objection not to criticize but to address the concern. The answer to all three questions is "no." The point of the chart is simply that some methods for reading the Bible are designed more for textual examination (#1) than for personal introspection (#2).

For centuries, attention has been given not only to methods that help evaluate and elucidate texts, but also to methods that assist in the care and feeding of the personal self. The chart merely helps to put these as they should be: side-by-side—joined.

Anyone interested in reading by the Spirit of God is certainly interested in both areas: text and self. Both sides have very specific methods for very specific things.[25] The sooner we learn this, the more quickly we are able to have meaningful conversations with biblical texts. *After all, we want to read biblical texts, not simply for **their** own sakes, and not simply for **our** own sakes, but ideally and ultimately for how the two intersect.*

As we go forward, we will talk about how these two areas relate to each other. We'll avoid the common claptrap of "I like this side" or "I like that one!"—as if one side is for eggheads and the other

---

[25] Some people have a misperception that reading the Bible "for what it means to me" somehow transcends all methods. Actually, this may signal a lack of disciplined reading that is more *selfish* than *for the self*.

for airheads. Rather, we want to see not only the need and value of both sides, but also why both sides need each other. For the sake of my ongoing illustration, each specific method (on either side) is like a specific dance. On the dance floor, different steps are needed for different types of music. Whereas we will not describe every kind of dance step, we will talk about the good, the bad, and the ugly of each side.

What's in a Name?

Let's begin by asking a question: "What does *Bible study* even mean?" Strange as that may sound, not everything that *calls* itself "Bible Study" *is*.

Unfortunately, this phrase gets attached to just about everything:

1. topical studies that bounce from text to text;
2. small groups that barely crack open a Bible;
3. pamphlets that might quote a single verse in a daily meditation;
4. light and airy devotional fly-overs of topics found in the Bible;
5. internet newsletters;
6. personal meditation on a given verse for "what this text means to me."

There's more, of course, and that's the problem: when everything is "Bible study," nothing is. It becomes a slogan that refers to just anything that might mention the Bible, even if remotely or barely.

However valuable the things listed above might be, confusing them with *Bible study* allows the tail (our goal) to wag the dog (the text) so that the phrase *Bible study* ends up meaning virtually anything anybody wants to do while holding a Bible.

Prime Directive

It is for that reason that I will, from this point on, often use the phrase *biblical text study* (instead of *Bible study*) as a way of emphasizing what is of prime interest. That is to say, it is my belief, practice, and constant emphasis when teaching, that, as much as humanly possible, the following is a prime directive:

> *Our primary concern when handling biblical texts is to respect and be guided by the purposes and intentions of those texts and their authors.*[26]

All approaches that call themselves "Bible Study" should seek to get in touch with that prime directive—and then stay in touch with it; it is both the starting point and parameters for all readings of biblical texts that would on any level call themselves "Bible study."

And I would call this a matter of decision and conscience: namely, to pursue a text for what it is overtly trying to do.

If we are not willing to stay in close touch with what the texts are trying to do, then like Paul in 1Cor 11:20 (where he says "It is not the *Lord's* supper you eat"), we should be clear that "It is not the *Bible* we are studying." The Bible is merely the diving board that we jump up and down on a few times, so we can jump into the pool of self-reflection. Now on a personal level, that might be a very valuable thing to do, but it is not *Bible* study.[27]

---

[26] I will speak below of what the text and/or the author is *trying to do or say*. When we respect the details of the text, that is how we respect the authors. So I will often talk about the two as one. For the details of this hotly debated topic, see Collier 2020.

[27] I specifically pursue this concept of *what a text is trying to do* in a detailed way in Collier 2020, chapter 4. First, *yes it is* possible, valid, and necessary to talk about textual intention in biblical documents, and I have dealt with complaints against this fully in that chapter. Second, biblical literature is far more complicated than a simple statement about "intention" can cover. This opens up a wide variety of possibilities for the value of multiple reading approaches—as long as it does not negate or displace the concern for what the text is overtly trying to do. Clearly, this may apply fluidly since different genres require different agendas. For example, the Song of Songs is not the same as a Pauline letter and may rightfully be open to a variety of reading agendas. No one "rule" applies to all biblical texts. Even so, it is possible to pursue the question "What is this text trying to do?" even within different genres.

I wish to emphasize strongly here that I am in no way belittling introspective or meditative interests—I will get to those next chapter. Instead, we need to keep the tail from wagging the dog. Clearly, we are going to have an array of specific interests, needs, and sensitivities depending on our immediate situation or state of mind. But anything that calls itself "Bible study" should be keenly interested in *what a text (i.e., a biblical author through a text) is trying to do.*[28]

The Bedpost Bible Study Method

It is well known that we can make the Bible say anything we like. In fact, it is always possible to use it for purposes other than what it was designed for and thereby to gain personal benefit from it.

As in the 1988 movie *Without a Clue.* Sherlock Holmes (Michael Caine) proclaims, "It's in the Bible! I have one at my bedside." So, running into his room, he reaches down to pull a Bible out from holding up the bedpost of an uneven bed.

He was using this Bible for a personal reason: to prop up his bed. Was it doing him any good? Yes! Did this have anything to do with the intent of any author in that book? Of course not.

People do this all the time: prop up their lives by using the Bible in all kinds of strained ways that have nothing to do with the intent of the authors. They use it as a book of magic, or secrets, or even worse, a club for beating other people over the head.

These are clearly abuses of biblical texts by people still fumbling around in the dark. It is like that verse in John:

"It had already grown dark, and Jesus had not yet come to them." (Jn 6:17)

This quote from John is not about the dangers of careless devotional Bible reading; it is about disciples of Jesus who are, at

---

[28] Even in texts that we don't know who the author is. Somebody wrote the text, and through that text we can, as readers, pursue what that text is trying to do.

that point, *still in the dark*. And in the Gospel of John, "dark" implies more than just nighttime.

Textual Study Methods

So we begin the process with textual study. Before we start asking "what does it mean to me," maybe we should ask, "What was it trying to say to them?" How do you feel when you are talking to a friend who continually twists your words into things you were not trying to say? Keep that in mind when reading the Bible.

Start with *textual study methods*. These methods focus on biblical texts themselves and especially on matters like context and intention.[29] Practical applications are of interest, but they do not dictate the terms of the study.

The Highs

A technical term for the close study of biblical texts is *exegesis*. Just like "*ex*it" means "to go out," *ex*egesis means "to lead out"— i.e., *to lead out* the meaning of any written text; to discover what a text meant in its original context. When you exegete a text, it means you pay close attention to the details of that text so as to learn what it meant.

This is not approached haphazardly or by the seat of one's pants. An *exegetical study* focuses on a given block of text within its larger context so as to learn what it means. Great attention is paid to the text itself, including vocabulary, grammar, argument, and the like. So, for example, 1Cor 10:4 says, "The Rock was Christ." When you study this, you might look up "rock" in various OT texts; and you will want to know how the phrase fits into 10:1-13, then chapters 8-10, and maybe the whole letter, or even all of Paul's letters.

---

[29] By *intention* I mean what an author was overtly *trying* to get at through a text. This is a highly debated topic. See Collier 2020 chapter 4 for a full discussion. As shorthand, I will also speak of what a *text* is trying to get at.

As *exegesis* studies texts closely, there are other textual methods related to exegesis that look at things like (1) the *history of textual traditions* that stand behind a text (such as how the theme "water from a rock" in two stories in Exodus and Numbers were developed and expanded in Jewish interpretation); or (2) how Paul's *rhetorical argumentation* might be related to other authors at that time. And so on, to many other specific methods, all designed for specific things.

There are many books on "how to study the Bible," but not all are of the same quality.[30] The methods of textual study can get very technical, and they can overwhelm anyone not trained in them. So, they are occasionally criticized as "nit-picking a text to death." But this is like criticizing carpenters for using too many nails when building a house. If you don't want the house to fall down, you might want to let the carpenters do their work. The same is true with biblical exegesis which aims to understand texts.

A simple way to define the goal of careful and responsible exegesis is that *exegesis seeks to discover what a text meant in its original context*. This *can* be used for highly academic interests. However, all Bible readers who want to grow in their handling of ancient biblical texts can learn appropriate steps that are not overly difficult.

For our purpose here, I point especially to two things: (1) a simple rule of thumb: treat a biblical text the way you want your own words to be treated; and (2) a general principle:

> *All efforts at biblical text study or exegesis can be just as Spirit-led as any other method.*
>
> *That's because people, not methods, are Spirit led.*

People sometimes reject exegesis as "too technical" and then they run over to "just reading by the Spirit." This means they don't understand either.

---

[30] Above all others, I highly recommend Fay 2013, Fee 2014, and Klein 2017.

associate Spirit-led reading with a particular approach is to turn Spirit-led reading into just another method. It is not a *method*; it is an *attitude of submission* to the Spirit of God—and this is applicable to any and all methods.

Stated another way, Spirit-led reading does not mean, "This is the method designed by the Spirit which you now have to follow!" It rather means that, regardless of the method(s) being used, all of them can be Spirit-led if the reader submits to the Spirit of God while using the methods responsibly.

So those who greatly admire biblical texts and respect them and want to learn more about and from them are happy to use exegetical and related methods because they focus first and foremost specifically on biblical texts. But the interest is never on *information* for information's sake; the interest is rather in gaining instruction: how texts function in context and what they are *trying* to do. Here biblical texts are read with more specific attention to literary structure, context, background history, archaeology, sociology, and numerous other concerns relevant for the study of biblical texts.

This type of reading of texts contextually is not purely academic; it is interested in and paves the way for the question "so what?" It allows us to become attentive to textual issues and to interact more responsibly with them.

The Lows

If we are not careful, the tail can wag the dog here. An exclusive focus on the *biblical text for the sake of text* can create readers who don't ever get around to asking "so what?" If our focus turns to "text for its own sake," this is unfortunate and can become merely an academic exercise. Academic concerns can be both important and useful. But when "biblical academics" becomes their own reason for existing (and this does happen), it's like going into a cave to dig for gold, and then forgetting to come out.

We begin with textual study to ask, "What was the author of this text trying to do?" It is a beginning, not an end.

5

Self

We certainly need to read the Bible for personal and lofty reasons—in search of *spiritual formation*. As with textual interests, there are methods that are applied to the *self*,[31] they are just not normally called methods; they are usually called *spiritual disciplines*.

Frankly, *disciplines* is a stellar designation that can now replace the word *methods* for both sides of our spectrum.

1	2
~~Methods~~ ***Disciplines for the Text:*** Used for textual and contextual evaluation and study	~~Methods~~ ***Disciplines for the Self:*** Used for personal introspection and contemplation

---

[31] I speak of "the self" or "our self" as used in psychology. See Baker 2020.

Contemplative Methods

These are disciplines of prayer, fasting, devotion, meditation, and spiritual Bible reading (e.g., *Lectio Divina*[32])—or even learning NT Greek as a spiritual discipline.[33] I have no intent in this book to describe or demonstrate these disciplines; rather, my aim is to present them together as a general class of methods that have *contemplative or introspective* spiritual goals. Most originated centuries ago, and they have received a great deal of valuable attention to this very day.[34]

The Highs

These methods can produce highly satisfying results—from the mildly encouraging to the sublime or breathtaking. They can bring us close to that magnificent verse:

> And the LORD used to speak to Moses "face to face," just like one might speak with a close friend.
> (Ex 33:11)

So then, as to the place and value of contemplative disciplines, we must recognize that these are all *specific methods* of reading. This may seem like an obvious point, but some people act (or outright claim) that these are anti-methods—written by the finger of God and now floating through the spiritual realms. But these are *methods—disciplines*—developed by and for human introspection. Clearly, there is tremendous, even life-giving value when approaching *anything* so introspectively: how may God be found in a night sky, a spider web, a sunset, a poem, a song, an experience, a book, a verse from the Koran—even a biblical text! I might be moved deeply by all of these, exclaiming earnestly, "Oh, how I am calmed, or invigorated, or convicted, or challenged!" I

---

[32] *Lectio Divina* is an emphasis growing out of monasteries on the prayerful reading of the Bible especially designed to promote communion with God.

[33] I've written about this at length already in Collier 2019, especially chapter 2.

[34] See short bibliography in Collier 2019, 123; or look up "Spiritual Formation" in Wikipedia for a reasonably good basic introduction.

might gain great personal insight in these ways, or find peace on any number of levels.

Contemplative methods, when properly pursued, can be incredibly beneficial for the self.

The Lows

But just like with textual approaches, the tail can wag the dog here as well. Approached irresponsibly, they can devolve into self-centered, ego-centric, and narcissistic Bible reading where the Spirit of God gets blamed for every personal whim. The more biblical texts are used in ways not intended by their authors, the easier it gets to twist and abuse those texts.

One woman inadvertently brought this clearly into view for me when she said:

> I don't really want to read the Bible for what it might have *meant*; and I don't want to study it and get all technical. I just want to read it for *what it means to me now!*

Clear warnings against this kind of selfish and self-centered Bible reading occur within biblical texts themselves, as when Jesus condemns the Pharisees for placing well-intended tradition about marriage and purity above what God intended with the law from the beginning (Matthew 5, 15, 19). Despite what many think, this is not so much about legalism as about self-centered (instead of God-centered) readings of the scriptures (as found in Deuteronomy 24). Even with good wishes, it is always possible to pervert the intentions of biblical texts into something we think we need now.

I have even heard some people say things like, "The Spirit of God shows me what I need to know now, no matter what Paul said!" Ok then, I get to play too: the Spirit of God is telling me now that this is an irresponsible way to read the Bible, and that it does not come from the Spirit!

For the Sake of People!

Now, occasionally, some feel uneasy with what I'm saying here, and some even get offended by it, as if I don't understand the aims or interests of the various contemplative disciplines, or as if I am denying the deep spiritual needs of people. But I like to reply with a very simple illustration: If you suddenly discover a box of old letters that your great-grand mother wrote to your mother, how much care will you give in reading them? Would you be at all concerned with what your great-grandmother was *trying* to say?

The question, here, is not "text vs. people?" It is rather, "What is the intention of a biblical text *for the sake of people?*" That was Jesus' concern against the Pharisees. His statement, "I desire mercy and not sacrifice," is not a statement of *people rather than law*; it is a statement of *law as intended by God for the sake of people!* We saw this also in the previous chapter for 2Corinthians 3.

Contemplative Methods are NOT!

Contemplative methods are not designed to discover what the text is trying to do. They might be like the fine tools used in finish-work when building a home (very important indeed!), but they are useless for digging the foundation, putting in the floor joists, putting up the walls, and putting on the roof.

In fact, the more we do contemplative readings *in concert with* what the texts are trying to do, the more powerful the results. (1) Textual disciplines and (2) contemplative disciplines should work hand-in-hand; one should never be used as "a replacement" for the other.

In our enthusiasm for spiritual transformation—truly a wonderful thing!—let us not turn the Bible into a prop for a short-legged bed.[35]

---

[35] An intentional echo of chapter 4.

DBS

Before moving to the next section, let's look at just one type of contemplative method: the *Discovery Bible Study* method *(DBS).*[36] Although "Bible Study" is in the name, this is a highly personal, "what it means to me" group experience that uses the Bible for personal reflection. There are four basic steps:

1. What's happening in my life?	**Can be**
2. *Bible text.*	**Spirit**
3. What does this mean to me?	**guided!**
4. Obey!	

Does this have any value? Of course it does! It can be inspiring, exciting, moving, meaningful, tear-jerking, or even calming! People cry, change their lives, or get highly motivated to act somehow. Can the Spirit use this method to transform people? Certainly!

Now, let's do something. Let's just replace "Bible text" in item 2 with anything else:

1. What's happening in my life?	**Can be**
2. *All you need is Love! (Beatles)*	**Spirit**
3. What does this mean to me?	**guided!**
4. Obey!	

Could this be a valuable, Spirit-led exercise? Yes! Is either one of these Bible study? No.

I'm not making fun of or "trashing" the approach, and I'm not saying that those who use this method put the Bible on the same level as a Beatles song. I'm just thinking about this for a minute.

*1. DBS is an intensely personalized method **using and reflecting on** the Bible.* It is not even trying to present itself (and that is fine) as a way to engage a biblical text on any kind of exegetical level; it

---

[36] https://www.dbsguide.org/

is about engaging our own hearts and lives *using* a biblical text or anything else (e.g., a song, a book, a poem, a sunset, a mountain top, etc.) as a *serious* sounding board. As outlined, it starts with me; it ends with me. It is mostly about me and what I can find in a text that I think applies to me and to the human race.

Can this be valuable? Of course it can! Certainly! As I have already made clear. If DBS brings people to the Bible on any level and gets them thinking and examining themselves, then great! I'm not being critical of that.

*2. But DBS is not **Bible** Study.* That does not make it bad, but it is not biblical text study. It encourages Bible reading, and of course that is good; but it's Bible reading from very specific *personal* perspectives and with highly personalized questions. Regardless of the name, this method of personal reflection by reading the Bible is not set up to explore or discover the nature, meaning, intent, or possible implications of specific biblical texts; what they were trying to accomplish, what they were claiming, how they are structured or argued. Without doubt, participants might have *opinions* about those things (just from reading), but this method, as a method, does not provide the kind of steps necessary to actually accomplish that. The method as outlined does not have that as a goal, and it would be incapable of accomplishing that even it wanted to. (It would be like using short finishing-nails to hold your roof in place—not a good idea!) That is not what this method is designed to do.

*3. Legitimate **biblical text** study does not start by focusing on me.*[37] Until I know what Paul is asking or addressing (or Matthew, or Genesis, etc.), I don't ever want to force my questions onto a text. Doing so will change the way I read it, understand it, and apply it.

Let's suppose, for example, that we run over to Genesis 1 with a question of our own, like: "How does this address the question of science and the Bible?" When that is how we *start,* there is little or no chance of reading Genesis on its own terms. We have

---

[37] The goal should be, as much as possible, to see from other perspectives.

already set ourselves up to see the text through our own question. So, if we actually came across the questions that Genesis is addressing, we likely would not understand or find them relevant.[38]

This same principle applies throughout the Bible with absolutely any text I (or you) can choose. If I start with a *me-centered method* of reading the Bible, I might find it very satisfying and enlightening, and I might feel closer to God; but I also might not be learning much at all from the Bible itself—except how to make it answer the questions that I want to ask.

Repertoire

The online Oxford Dictionary, *Lexico*, defines the word *repertoire* like this:

> *A stock of plays, dances, or pieces that a company or a performer knows or is prepared to perform.*

When it comes to dancing with the Bible, an array of disciplines (methods) in two categories is available, depending on the text and specific need.

REPERTOIRE OF DISCIPLINES FOR BIBLE READING	
Disciplines for the Text	**Disciplines for the Self**
✓ Text Study ✓ Exegesis ✓ Academic methods (numerous) ✓ etc.	✓ Devotion ✓ Meditation ✓ Sing/Pray Scriptures ✓ Lectio Divina ✓ etc.

Table 1: Disciplines

---

[38] At *IABC* we have a 14-week recorded class on Genesis 1-11, and we deal with this in detail.

Energetic Bible readers will never be satisfied with one-sided readings of the Bible. And they will know:

1. *Methods are not Spirit-led, people are.*
2. *Disciplines help us read biblical texts responsibly to feed our souls.*
3. *Text is for the sake of people, not over people.*
4. *I have mentioned only a few disciplines.*

Ready, now, for Conversation

Chapter 1 introduced the tantalizing idea of *Biblical Conversation* and painted a brief portrait of what *could be* when reading the Bible.

Chapter 2 pointed out that the word *conversation* is not used by virtually anybody to describe reading the Bible. Readers are often treated or depicted as outsiders to a text rather than as participants in the text, and this has contributed to the idea that "Spirit-led Bible reading" is some kind of super anti-method against all methods.

Chapters 3-5 explode this myth with a balanced repertoire of disciplines for both text and self.

The disciplines help us dance with texts and self. This makes possible a new skill: *intimate conversation.* Here, readers become *conversation partners* in one of the greatest ongoing conversations the world has ever known.

PART 2:
JOURNEY

Biblical Conversation
is an artful encounter with biblical texts.
It treats them,
not as mere objects to be read,
but as living conversation partners to be engaged.

Here we take a few steps
on a Journey into the inter-biblical conversations
that occur throughout our biblical texts.

First,
we'll notice various shades of conversation
in our biblical texts;
and then
we'll walk with Paul
through only one such encounter.

This will give us a taste.

6

Shades of Conversation

We are now ready for conversation. But that doesn't mean "start talking!" It means "close your mouth and start listening!" So we turn first to biblical texts.

Since chapter 1, we have been using two illustrations for *Biblical Conversation*: (1) how *biblical authors engage each other* in ongoing conversation (Jesus, Moses, Elijah); and (2) how *we keep that conversation going in ourselves* (Jacob wrestling with God). All of Part 2 (chapters 6-8) will focus on the first: *how biblical authors engage each other.*[39]

This is crucial. Unless we get down into the texts and see with our own eyes how biblical authors engage each other, the phrase *biblical conversation* will simply mean "gabbing with each other about the Bible." *Biblical* conversation must arise out of *biblical* texts.

A warning: these chapters might challenge you! They might very well slow you down. They should! You certainly will need to sit up straight, open your Bible, and engage in the process. If you

---

[39] The second concern will be picked up in Part 3.

don't do that, it is quite possible you will simply not understand what *Biblical Conversation* is all about.

Shades

Biblical Conversation comes in three different shades. All three of these are *conversation*, just different shades of it (different kinds or levels of it). No one would say that when I talk with you it is the same as when I talk with God during prayer. We readily recognize that these are different kinds of conversations. Shades 1 and 2 are easily recognizable.

(S1) **Shade 1** = talking to each other in person, by letters, etc.
(S2) **Shade 2** = praying to or interacting directly w/ God
(S3) **Shade 3** = authors interactively engaging previous authors and texts to encounter God; this includes our own efforts to join in.

Table 2: Shades

Shades 1 & 2

Shade 1: Normal Conversations

It is fair and proper to speak of some NT letters (like 1Thessalonians) as a part of a *normal conversation* (i.e., an S1).[40] We have a live author (Paul) who is carrying on a live conversation with live conversation partners—whether face to face or by letter. Paul is engaging his readers on a personal level.

Shade 2: Prayer as Conversation

In addition to normal conversation(S1), we can just as appropriately speak of *Shade 2 Conversation* (S2) in 1Thessalonians. Paul focuses a great deal on speaking with God. From his opening words: "When I talk to God" (1:2), to his two

---

[40] See Collier 2020 chapters 10 and 11 for a much more detailed discussion of the nature and form of NT letters, especially 1Thessalonians.

major "wish prayers (3:11-13 and 5:23-24), to his final words: "May the grace of our Lord Jesus Christ be with you" (5:28), and to other places where prayer is sought, assumed, or encouraged—this is more than S1 human conversation.

Shades 1 & 2 in Biblical Texts

S1 & S2 conversations are common throughout the Bible. They tend to be one on one.

In **Genesis** 1 and 2, the man and his wife are in the garden when God immediately and literally strikes up a conversation. God calls out, "Where are you?" The man replies, "I was naked and afraid, and I hid myself." And God asks, "Who told you that?" And on it goes. The story is told in terms of a living conversation in which God carries on a somewhat pointed dialog with both Adam and Eve. The story implies an open and ongoing relationship between God and his newest and closest creation, including conversation.

This was not a democracy, not by any stretch; and God wasn't asking for Adam's advice on what to do next. But in a context of distant and cruel gods, the God of Adam and Eve is shown not to be harsh, stone-faced, or distant; he is rather near, walking with them in the garden and ready for interaction.[41]

In fact, Genesis overflows with such a characterization. A live, active conversation ensues with Cain, Noah, Abram/Abraham, Hagar, Sarah, and Jacob. These were not just "do as I say" moments; these are presented as times of questions, of bargaining, of laughter, of concern, of eating, and even of pleading—on the part of both man and God.

In **Exodus** the conversations between God and Moses are presented in detail and as major events. And the point? God did not just shout the laws from a mountain top (as in some Star Trek episode, with a booming, menacing, male voice). Conversation is

---

[41] Yes, of course, there is more to this story, but I am after the point of the presentation of conversation, here. Nothing else.

embedded in the Law. *The* Ten Commandments came into being amid conversation, God with Moses.

S1 & S2 conversations are embedded in **the Pentateuch**. From the magnificent interchange at the burning bush, to the confrontations with Pharaoh, to the sea, to the mountain of the Lord, to the golden calf, to the daily frustrations of administration, to bringing forth of water, to the final sermons delivered in Deuteronomy—*it is all in the context of an ongoing conversation with God.* And so, it is said of Moses:

> The LORD would speak to Moses face to face, the way a person speaks to a friend. (Ex 33:11; cf. Gen 32:30; Num 11:16f; Dt 5:4; 34:10)

The overt claim of conversation with Moses is both explicit and pervasive. And this understanding would not be forgotten. It would echo in the book of **Sirach** 45:1-5 (written 200-175 BCE) which lauds and extols Moses in the highest terms: "a man of mercy . . . beloved by God and man . . . equal in glory to the holy ones . . . [God] glorified him . . . gave him commands . . . showed him part of his glory . . . sanctified him . . . chose him." And then this:

> God made him hear his voice,
> > and led him into the thick darkness,
> and gave him the commandments *face to face*,
> > the law of life and knowledge,
> to teach Jacob the covenant,
> > and Israel his judgments.

God came to him *personally* and *up close*, in the spirit of Ex 33:11.

Such a representation of S1 & S2 dialog continues **beyond the Pentateuch** with significant conversations represented between God and Joshua, the people, Gideon, Manoah, Samuel, David, Solomon, Isaiah, Jeremiah, Ezekiel, Hosea, Jonah, and others. Even the Psalms (which are, at base, prayers)[42] are a direct, open,

---

[42] Brueggemann 2000, 1, writes: "The Psalms are helpful because they are a genuinely dialogical literature that expresses both sides of the conversation of faith. On the one hand, Israel's faithful speech addressed to God is the substance of the Psalms. The Psalms do this so

and explicit talking to God. In all of these, God's position is always that of a faithful and just God who loves and cares for his people and who is clearly the greater party in the interchange. Nevertheless, with everything they ask, write, and inquire, they are *in conversation with* God.

The same is found especially of many of the stories in the Gospels/Acts and in the letters of the **New Testament**. Acts 15 is especially useful. This story illustrates incredibly well a principle: *"Biblical writers, and all early church leaders, were **in conversation with one another** as they were collectively, all the while, **in search of a conversation with God**."* This point is specifically stated and stressed in the story.

> "For it has seemed good to the Holy Spirit and to us . . ."
> Acts 15:28 RSV

In addition to the speeches themselves, the phrase, "It seemed good to us," appears twice in the chapter: vv. 25 and 28. There was definitely a serious conversation going on between these people about what to do. Nothing before had been written about this situation. Some will say that they, on their own, made the first decision (v. 25), and the Holy Spirit made the second (v. 28). But this misses the point of the story. The Spirit is alive and working in the midst of all the chaos, in all the genuine efforts to find the will of God—and it happens as the people of God *engage each other*. The implication of the story is that the Spirit worked through the chaos of the intense human conversation—as they labored together to know what step to take.

There is much more, of course, but it is fairly clear: Jewish and Christian sacred texts overtly include live, ongoing, actual S1 & S2 conversations.

---

fully and so well because they articulate the entire gamut of Israel's speech to God, from profound praise to the utterance of unspeakable anger and doubt" (my italics, gdc).

Shade 3: Authors in Community

Shade 3 conversation (S3) is a bit more involved. In essence, this is *authors in conversation with each other over time for the sake of a struggling, unrelenting community.* In biblical texts, we get to witness this conversation up close:

1. We watch a biblical author (like Paul) deal with his own new situation by engaging earlier authors through their texts (e.g., Moses, Isaiah, Jeremiah).

   a. We watch as those earlier authors are speaking to their own contexts through their texts.

   b. We watch how our current author understands, interprets, adapts, updates and/or changes, and applies the earlier authors to new situations.

   c. In this way, we get to see how our biblical author is *in conversation with* earlier authors through their texts.

2. Hence, as Paul is *walking around* among earlier authors and texts, those *earlier authors* continue to live in those texts, and they are alive for Paul.

Paul is not simply quoting some old dead text; this is a *community conversation—ongoing, enduring for years or centuries—in search of a conversation with God.* And this is how God works through community to give us our sacred texts: they emerge as living texts from deep-level S3 conversations.

Shade 3 conversation goes beyond the normal uses of that term, and this is why it is difficult for some to grasp it: they have never heard of it before—at least not, in relation to the Bible.

But there is nothing new about this; it is well known in our own time. The word *conversation* is routinely used for how ideologies interact: literature is said to be in conversation with politics, or religion with science, or works of art with literature. So "being in conversation with" something is a common phrase that can denote even inanimate objects. One thing is said to have influenced another, sometimes in subtle ways, but often in startling ways.

Shade 3 conversations are a common and formative part of our biblical texts.

What Conversation Does Not Mean

So then, by saying Paul "interacts with" or Paul is "in conversation with" a text, I don't simply mean "he **reads**" since it is possible to read something and stay on the fringes of it; I don't mean "he **encounters**" since that often connotes something unexpected, unpleasant, or even unseemly and would depict the author pretty much without initiative (as in "he encounters a stranger in a dark alley"); I don't mean "he **uses** the OT," no matter how common that phrase is, since it is not a very happy expression (it is rather like "using your wife" to fix your supper); I don't mean "he **listens** to" (as a dutiful student listens to a teacher), although this is getting better since listening is a huge part of what is happening; and I also don't just mean "he **interprets.**" Even though this is technically a part of what he is doing, this last word is somewhat "flat": not very picturesque, and not much able to open one's eyes to the *excitement of interchange* that is taking place.

I mean something more than all of these: something that reaches in and gets a handful of the *wonder* that is happening during the interchange; something that catches Paul as author and interpreter in the very act of an interpretive event as he pursues a give-and-take with someone before him. I mean not only uncovering the dynamics and mechanics of how the author quotes, alludes to, or echoes texts, but also feeling his heart as he eagerly listens to and then hungrily questions those texts; how he *midrashically*[43] engages Moses or Isaiah or Jeremiah or the Psalmist. At such times, *he is "in conversation with" them!*

---

[43] For Midrash the present book see pp. 39 and 91.

Let's be clear: When describing what Paul is doing at such times, I am not even *trying* to talk about S1 or S2 "conversation." Dictionary definitions don't fit here. I'm talking about a whole 'nother shade of it, where Paul is *interacting with* those who came before—*conversing with them by engaging them through their texts.*

Ready, Set . . .

We are now ready for a close look as a specific example: Water in the Desert: a nation-building story told over centuries, from Israel, to Judaism, and to Paul (chapters 7 and 8).

A warning: These chapters get a little more detailed. No apologies. This is classic *Biblical Conversation*—the heart of this book.

— 7 —

Water
in the Desert

You've reached the heart of the book. If you like biblical texts, you'll love this part.

A single concrete example will illustrate the principles I'm setting forth. This example is one of the best in all of Paul or even the NT, and it will illustrate the kind of thing going on in many other NT texts.

It starts a long time ago—long before Paul was born; way back in the earliest parts of the OT: Ex 17:1-7 and Num 20:1-11. It will help if you treat this like a personal Biblical text study. Read both texts and keep them open before you.

Water from the Rock

These stories look curiously like a doublet (the same story told twice). Are they? They are told as separate stories (two occurrences) in two different locations: Exodus 17 at Rephidim in the Wilderness of Sin, and Numbers 20 at Kadesh in the

Wilderness of Zin.[44] The author(s) clearly present(s) them as two events, but are they two versions of the same story?

[A quick aside: I have to get just a little bit technical here for a minute, but I hope you will stay with this. It will illustrate not only that biblical texts are not made out of the cotton candy that many devotional books or sermons seem to assume, it will also demonstrate how biblical texts—especially OT texts—are written from the time of their earliest oral beginnings out of deep-level, ongoing oral and written conversations. This is not something to dread; it is a rather amazing reality to discover about biblical texts—that they originate from an ongoing, deep-level conversational search for God!]

Back, now, to our two stories: Both associate Meribah ("place of strife") with their story, since "they contended with the LORD" (Ex 17:7 and Num 20:13). The bulk of biblical scholarship has assumed this to be one story told twice.[45] Ex 17:1-7 has often been regarded as an *interweaving of various traditions* (JE),[46] written to explain the origin of Meribah.[47]

[Stop again! Ok, so I'm already in trouble with some readers, by even talking about the interweaving of traditions, because they think somehow that this detracts from the special character of the books. But conservative reactions against the idea of multiple sources in biblical texts are overdone. Long ago, some scholars were simply trying to explain the apparent and real differences of style in Genesis-Deuteronomy, and they came up with a suggestion: JEPD. This is a now common listing of four separate proposed sources from which the current form of the Pentateuch was constructed: **J**ahwist, **E**lohist, **P**riestly, and **D**euteronomist. This was the product of Source Criticism in the late 19th and early 20th centuries, and it looked for signs of layers of source material

---

[44] Two of the seven wildernesses crossed by the Israelites: Shur, Etham, Sin, Sinai, Paran, Zin, and Kadesh.

[45] Keil 1869, 132 repudiates the notion altogether as having "no firm ground whatever"; see also Wenham 1981, 149-50. For those who support the view see among others Gray 1903, 258-59; Driver 1911, 154-58; Noth 1962, 137-40; Noth 1968, 143-47; Hyatt 1971, 179-82; and Childs 1974, 305-09.

[46] A source called "J" by scholars, and a source called "E", now combined.

[47] Noth 1962, 139; Hyatt 1971. But see Childs' statement: "The tradition did not develop from the etiology [i.e., why the story was told], but this etiology subsequently attached itself to the tradition of Yahweh's aid in the wilderness" Childs 1974, 307.

that make up the Pentateuch. The original theory is certainly out of favor now among scholars. But the idea is still discussed because there are obvious differences in style and also evidence of editing hands within the Pentateuch, whether those sources were written or oral.[48]

Despite objections by some, this not only does not destroy anything about the Bible (except maybe some poorly formed theories about it), it actually makes a whole lot of sense; namely, that 3,000 years ago, the Pentateuch was a *pulling together* of many stories that were already sacred to its people—nation-building stories that were deep in conversation with each other!]

Now back to our stories again: maybe the Exodus 17 and Numbers 21 stories were in conversation with each other. In fact, Ex 17:1-7 has often been regarded as an *interweaving of various traditions* (JE),[49] written to explain the origin of Meribah;[50] and Num 20:1-13 has often been seen as a reworking of Exodus 17 to explain the exclusion of Moses and Aaron from Canaan. For example, Martin Noth comments on the Numbers text:

> P [the Priestly editor] has consciously altered this tradition of the water-miracle as it appears in its original JE form in Exodus 17 in view of the purpose with which this story is told in P.[51]

Now I already know that some have closed this book just for these comments. But, honestly, whether one likes the whole "source" approach (JEPD) for understanding the Pentateuch is quite immaterial. For whether we can precisely trace the traditions or not, it is fairly apparent that a good deal of "*community*

---

[48] Those who criticize the idea do not pay attention to the claims in the texts themselves. That later editors had a hand in this is specifically claimed in the oft-repeated phrase: "to this day" in Gen 19:37, 38; 22:14; 26:33; 32:32; 35:20; 47:26; 48:15; Ex 10:6; Num 22:30; Dt 3:22; 3:14; 10:8; 11:4; 29:4; 34:6; also, the fact that Dt 32:1ff overtly recounts the story of Moses' death from an outside position; and so many other examples. Any decent "Introduction to the Old Testament" will list such things.

[49] Essentially, all of this notion of sources (JEPD) simply means that scholars were trying to evaluate the Pentateuch based on vocabulary, language style, and the like, and came to believe that it actually was composed of several major oral or written sources that originally existed on their own. Someone (or some group) brought these together into a single, unified story: Genesis through Deuteronomy.

[50] See above, fn. 46.

[51] Noth 1968, 146. Cf. also Gray 1903, 258-59 for an attempt at a detailed reconstruction of the original traditions.

conversation" (i.e., development of older traditions) has gone on prior to this point for either text. Brevard Childs, for example (famous for his "canonical" approach to the OT), is not so eager to "trace the tradition," but still acknowledges the obvious "*traditions backdrop*" for Ex 17:1-7:

> There is such a variety in the Old Testament's use of the Meribah tradition that one can suspect a *complete history of tradition*[52] lying behind the present narrative. Unfortunately the evidence for tracing this development is no longer available, and one is left with a variety of hypotheses which have little chance of being established or disproved.[53]

The existence of oral/written traditions behind the Exodus story is assumed by nearly all scholars, and it makes a great deal of sense, based on everything we can see. Furthermore, on a close look, Num 20:1-10 does, in fact, look like a revision of Ex 17:1-7 (or both stories a revision of something earlier). The two accounts are so similar that, taking only the common elements, one finds a perfectly coherent kernel:[54]

> And the whole congregation of the sons of Israel [journeyed from one place to another] and there was no water. And the people found fault with Moses saying, "Why have you brought us up from Egypt to kill us and our livestock? We need water. And Yahweh said to Moses, 'Take the rod and [do something with the congregation] and [take someone with you] and [do something to the rock] and water will go out from it that the people may drink.' And Moses [responded in some way to the words of the Lord]. This place is called Meribah where the sons of Israel found fault.

[52] This is shorthand for a lot of previous traditions, oral and/or written, at various stages being brought together.
[53] Childs 1974, 306 (my italics, gdc). Childs makes this statement after reviewing various attempts to define sources behind Exodus 17 (Hyatt and Gressmann = two complete strands; Noth = J, v. 3 E; Fritz = P; Rudolph = J; Coats = oral tradition). His caution seems altogether warranted.
[54] I'm not suggesting this as "the original"; I'm merely showing how similar they are. Brackets [..] indicate contradictory material between the *texts* which nevertheless have a common element. That common element is stated within the brackets. Underscored words indicate differences between the two *texts* of specific wording only, the concept being the *same*.

In fact, the *additions* found in either story make perfect sense when seen in light of the purpose that each story was telling in each context. This is very much like two preachers telling the same Bible story to two different groups of people on two different occasions. You can bet there will be some subtle terminology changes, or details emphasized, or commentary added to each story based on the overriding goal at the time.

With your Bible open, look at your texts now:

(1) *Ex 17:1-7 is about the* **presence** *of Yahweh.* The final question identifies the main point: "Is Yahweh *present* with us or not?" In this story, "the rod with which you struck the Nile" recalls the presence and power of Yahweh in Egypt. And his "standing" on the rock (MT עֹמֵד|*'omēd* and LXX ἕστηκα|*hestēka*)[55]—God, not the rock, is the source of their water. In Exodus 17 "water from the rock" *functions* to show Yahweh's presence.

(2) *Num 20:1-13 is about the* **holiness** *of Yahweh* (vv, 6, 12, 13). So the rod is important for different reasons in Numbers 20. Here the rod is described as Aaron's rod which budded (Num 17:16-26 MT & LXX; 17:1-11 English), a rod which showed the holiness or separateness of Aaron (i.e., the tribe of Levi) as God's chosen one. However, the subtle change of focus to the holiness of God by way of Moses' sin of rebellion also alters the import of the water-yielding rock. It now assumes a lesser role in the account, and in this text it does not point to God's presence![56]

---

[55] Yahweh "stands" in Isa. 3:13 as a sign of his authority to judge: "Yahweh has taken his place to contend/and stands to judge his people"; in Ex 17:6 relates to his presence among the people. The action here is not a judgment, but a show of presence.

[56] There are many other things to see in a comparison of the two texts. Only in Num 20:1-13 is Moses' striking the rock stated in connection with his sin though "striking the rock" is never named as the sin. Psa. 78:20 "He struck the rock so that water gushed out"; Psa. 106:32-33 notes that it went badly for Moses for "the words he spoke rashly," but striking the rock is not mentioned. In Ex 17:1-7, the possible wordplay between *nasa'* "test" (*vv.* 2, 7) and *naca'* "strike" (*vv.* 5, 6) points to the presence of Yahweh. Their "testing" of Yahweh was sinful; but through "striking" the rock, his presence was vindicated: "they tested him saying, 'Is he present with us or not?'" In Num 14:12ff, a similar wordplay occurs: Because Israel tested (*nasa'*) God, God struck (*naca'*) them. Admittedly this is a different application, but the wordplay is present all the same. Num 20:1-13, however, does not have the word "test," eliminating the word-play of Exodus 17. Even if Numbers 20 is not a reworking of Exodus 17, the absence of "test" along with other differences changes the focus from the presence of Yahweh to his holiness in contrast to the sin of

75

Those elements which emphasize the presence of Yahweh in Exodus 17 are the very ones missing in Numbers 20, while the elements in Numbers 20 emphasizing the holiness of Yahweh are absent from Exodus 17. Whether one argues that these are two separate historical accounts or two literary retellings of a single tradition, one must deal with this fact: *at the heart of both accounts is an identical kernel which is applied differently in each context.* What we have is a story-form from earliest Israel that is *adaptable* within community conversation—an *adaptability* that is already at work in the earliest documents of the Jewish sacred texts. **This is a very early example of conversation at work in biblical texts.** And this conversation will attract and continue to inspire and shape later sacred conversations with these ideas, even into the NT. But the conversation is just getting started.

Well, Well, Well

Now comes another prominent early text, **Num 21:17**. This is a song about a well: "Spring up, O well! Give it song . . ." Here is a separate story that appears to have no connection to the water from the rock of either **Exodus 17** or **Numbers 20**.

But it does not stay separate for long. For when the tradition "*water in the desert*" is traced through the Jewish scriptures and beyond, we see how a tradition begins to take on "a life of its own" in Hebrew, Greek, and Aramaic literature, sometimes based on wordplays, other word associations, or word connections.

Allow me to illustrate. . . and hold on to your hat!

(1) *There is a clear progression of thought that takes place within the Jewish scriptures themselves.* From a **rock** (in Ex 17 and Num 20[57]) and a **well** (in Num 21), other texts begin to *conflate* (co-mingled, mix together) these earlier stories into a single,

---

Moses—insubordination was the sin (cf. Num 20:24 "rebellion"), striking the rock was not the sin. More in Collier 1994.

[57] It is normal to spell out a book and chapter when no verses are mentioned (Exodus 17, Numbers 20, etc.). But because of numerous references in this section, I will use shorthand: Ex 17, Num 20, Num 21.

generalized story about water in the desert. That, all by itself, is an interpretational move. Two examples:

(a) Some OT texts *idealize* this story to laud the wonderful and continuing grace of God (as God had cared for Israel "back then" in the desert, God still cares for us now).[58]

(b) Other OT texts *re-actualize* (retell, but update for a new situation) the story to indicate either

(i) "a new exodus" of Israel from bondage[59] or
(ii) "the good life."[60]

These are all expansions beyond the original meanings and are the result of *live, ongoing, developing community conversations* about God who is continually at work for their sake. And these various developments spur-on all subsequent Jewish and Christian enhancements of the story of water in the desert—as we will now see.

(2) Rabbinic texts, for example, do something rather amazing with the entire collection of these biblical stories—something that no OT text does: *they start talking about a well that **followed Israel** through the desert!* [61] And why not: the biblical texts already were lauding that everywhere Israel went God gave them water (e.g., Neh 9:15-20 in a highly generalized context). So, Jewish interpreters don't just make this up out of thin air; they develop the idea of a *following* well by joining in on a conversation already going on within biblical texts. Even prior to the time of Paul, they begin to tell some incredible stories about this following well.

But where do they get a "following well?" Jewish interpreters, knowing how biblical texts already idealize and reactualize the "water in the desert" theme, now home in on one particular text: **Num 21:17-20.** This text then is seen as a key for explaining all

---

[58] See, e.g., Psalms 78, 105, and 119; Dt 8:15-16; and Neh. 9:6-37.
[59] Isa. 35:6-7; 41:17-20; 43:16-21; 49:10; and especially 48:17-22 (LXX).
[60] Dt 32:13-14; Psalm 81:17; Job 20:17; 29·6.
[61] Among many others, see *Tg. Ps. -J.* Num. 20:1-13; 21:16-17; *Tg. Neof.* Num. 21:19; *Num. R.* I.2; XIX.25-26, *Midr. Tehillim* 105. More in Collier 1994..

other water texts throughout the Jewish scriptures, including Ex 17 and Num 20.

Num 21:17-20 says:

[17] Spring up, O well! Give it song . . .
[18] And from the wilderness they went on to **Mattanah**,
[19] and from **Mattanah to Nachaliel**,
and from **Nachaliel to Bamoth**,
[20] and from **Bamoth** to the **valley** lying below

The words in bold are place names. But the early Jewish interpreters prior to Paul or Jesus did not merely *read* the text, they *interacted* with it. So since the place names can be read to mean, respectively, "**gift, rivers,** and **height**," this allowed *Targum Onqelos* (in the late 1st century or early 2nd century CE [62] to say:

[the well] **was given** to them in the wilderness. And . . . it descended with them to **the rivers**, and from the rivers it went up with them to **the height**, and from the height to the **valley** which is in the fields of Moab. [63]

In other words, it followed them everywhere! Based on wordplays,[64] this is understood to mean more than place names; it also describes—on some deeper level—the travels of this well. So now, other water texts are able to be read along with this one, until rabbinic texts begin to describe this well as "**rock-shaped," like a beehive** that rolled around during the travels of the Israelites in the desert giving them water.[65]

---

[62] CE = Common Era, replaces AD; BCE = Before Common Era, replaces BC.

[63] *Tg. Onq.* Num 21:18-19 (trans. by Etheridge 1865, 302). The bolded words have been interpreted: Matanah, "given"; Nachaliel, taken as *nachal*, "river"; and Bamoth, "height."

[64] Wordplays and puns in English are common. What did the ram say to his wife? "I love ewe." What did the mayonnaise say when the girl opened the fridge door? Close the door, I'm dressing!" Wordplays in biblical texts might be humorous, but they were more often a serious way to link ideas or even texts from different locations. In chapter 1, we noted the wordplay between "wrestle" (*yēobēq*), the river "Jabbok" (*yabboq*), and the name Jacob (*ya'āqob* "one who contends"). This helps to emphasize the notion of "contending" in that story. There are many like this. In the current text, the wordplays become a much more serious way of liking and interpreting one text by another the same or similar words.

[65] *Tg. Ps.-J* Num. 21:16-17. Cf. also *Tg. Neof.* Num. 21:19. "And since the well (namely the rock well) was given to them as a gift, it became strong overflowing streams, and it ascended to the top of the mountains and went down with them to the deep valleys" (as translated by A. Diez Macho 1960, 23lff.). See also *Num. R.* I.2 (ET, 1:5). *Num. R.* XIX.25-26 (ET, II:774-777)." More in Collier 1994.

Even a small adjustment in a word (such as from *nachaliel* to *nachal* to *nahal*—a change as subtle as a single Hebrew letter, from ה to ח —look carefully) can lead to major changes in understandings.[66] So these words can be taken literally (as place names), or they can be read in other ways by ancient interpreters, and they would all be considered completely legitimate understandings.[67]

1. For example, as already shown, some read these words as directions showing all the places the well followed Israel in the desert to give them water.

2. But in another text,[68] the three place names of Num 21 are seen to correspond "to the three courts of law in Jerusalem, which explained the Torah to Israel."

3. And in another text still,[69] the phrase explains the statement "he that occupies himself in the study of the law shall be exalted." The Law, which is the "gift" (*matanah*) from God, "leads" (understanding *nachaliel* as *nahal* "lead" rather than *nachal* "river") one to the "height" (Bamoth). And so, it exalts the one who studies.

Again, these were not considered as competing or contradictory interpretations; they were seen as equally valid readings showing deeper insights into the mind of God. This was a *community conversation* that was developing over centuries and generations.

---

[66] Cf. also Philo in *Det.* 114-18.

[67] That is why a late rabbi, Ena (ca. 515 CE), could associate the water flowing abundantly from beneath the Temple in Ezek. 47:1-12 with Isa. 12:3: "Therefore with joy shall ye draw water from the wells of salvation" (BT, *Sukkah* 48b [ET, 227]); and why the Tosefta could associate the same Ezekiel text to the well dug by princes in Num. 21 now said to be waters from "a great river, pouring themselves into the Mediterranean, and bringing thence all the precious things of the world," (Tosefta, *Sukkah* 111, 11-13). These may be late statements, but the agenda of connecting similar water texts to extol the abundance of God's grace is not late at all. (Cf. e.g., Ezek. 47:1-12; Jn. 7:37 and 8:12.)

[68] *Num. R.*, XIX.26 (ET, 1:776)

[69] *'Abot* 6.2 (ET, Danby 1933, 459)

(3) Other ancient Jewish texts show this to be a widespread idea. For example, *Pseudo-Philo,*[70] (likely 2nd century CE,[71]) clearly *does* refer to the "following well" found in rabbinic texts.[72]

So after all is said and done, this much should be clearly understood: *Interpretations and developing traditions within communities of faith are nothing less than conversations with sacred texts and previous traditions; and these conversations show up in the details of wordplays and other acts of interpretation.*

To help show all of this, the figure below offers a mere illustration of interpretive movement and relationships. The

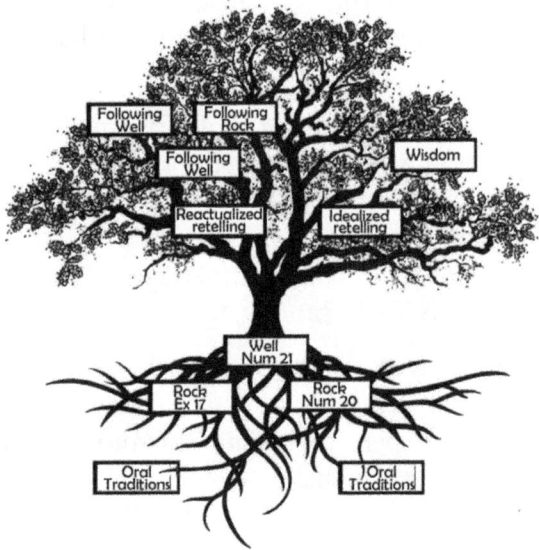

Figure 3: Conversation Tree

---

[70] *Bib. Ant.* 10:7; 11:15.

[71] Jacobson 1996, 201, the major commentator of Pseudo-Philo, dates it to about 150 CE.

[72] The *Wisdom of Solomon* and *Philo* are written by pre-Pauline Hellenistic Jews, and neither makes a reference to a following well. Instead, both build mostly on the kinds of expansions found within OT texts themselves. For example, **Wis** 11:1-15 idealizes the "water from the rock" tradition to show the exaltation of Israel over Egypt. (Cf. 10:15 where Israel is referred to as a "blameless race.") In 11:4, no text is quoted, though several are echoed. For a detailed analysis of Wisdom 11-19, see Wright 1965. **Philo** deals with the various OT texts in both a straightforward manner (*Mos.* 1:181, 191, 210-11, 255-56; *Decal.* 16) and a thoroughgoing allegorical manner (*Somn.* 2:221-22, 270-71; *Ebr.* 112-13; and esp. *Leg.* 2:86-87 and *Det.* 114-118). See also Philo *Conf.* 138; *Leg.* 3:4, 169; *Migr.* 183; *Sacr.* 67; *Somn.* 1:241. Philo is especially fond of interpreting both Num 21:18-19 and Dt 32:13 allegorically as the source of Wisdom. Especially *Det.* 114-118.

process begins with the roots of oral or written sacred tradition, and then moves up the trunk to the branches. Each step sees an adaption of what went before for new situations. This tree shows two major branches or conversations: the left and right. In reality, the applications (branches) would be more complicated.

Now, as Christian readers, we might be tempted by all of the teaching we have received literally not to care about ancient Jewish writings like *Targum Onqelos* or *Pseudo-Philo*, or any other ancient document that is not already in the Bible. But in that case, how would we explain what happens in Paul?

Next Up

So, to give a preview of the next chapter: When Paul talks about a *following rock* in 1Cor 10:4, he does not get this from any OT text; instead, he is *in conversation with* the many OT texts that speak of water in the desert *as they have long ago come to be understood through earlier Jewish conversations about those texts.* In other words, he is talking the language that anyone near a Synagogue would understand.[73]

We will get into this more, starting now.

---

[73] Sometimes commentators will fall all over themselves to rescue Paul from referring to a Jewish legend about a following well. They might claim that Paul could have arrived at the idea of a "following" water source all by himself. But this is more than a bit nonsensical, and it treats Paul as if he was ignorant of what Jewish interpreters were doing with these texts before he was born. Clearly, Paul is reflecting awareness of this ongoing Jewish conversation. But when Paul enters the conversation, he brings to it Jesus Christ. So now, he redirects that conversation to Christ as the rock. See next chapter.

_8_

Paul
in Conversation

Enter Paul into this longstanding, vibrant, and growing
conversation. Whether or not any of this "following well"
information is new to us, he inherited it from birth. However—
and this is key—he does not simply repeat what he has heard. Paul
himself now enters the conversation, adapts it, and helps to
develop it in a new direction: a direction that flows from Christ.

This Rock

When Paul is ready to laud how God had provided water in the
desert, he retells the story in the traditional terms of the "following
well" (from the previous chapter), only now he focuses on the
LORD who was present in the rock in Exodus 17, especially as that
gets retold in texts like Deuteronomy 32, Psalm 78, Nehemiah 9
and many others. And he retells this story in what appears to be
something like a Christ-based synagogue sermon.

> ¹For I do not want you to be ignorant, brothers and sisters, that our ancestors
>> all were under the cloud, and
>> all passed through the sea; ²and
>> all were baptized into Moses
>>> in the cloud and in the sea; ³and
>> all ate the same spiritual food, ⁴and
>> all drank the same spiritual drink.
>>> For they used to drink from
>>> the spiritual following rock.
>>> Now, this Rock . . . it was Christ! ⁵
> But with most of them God was not pleased,
> for they were scattered all over the desert.

1Cor 10:1-5

With this opening comment, Paul is calling to mind a common story told in synagogue sermons (perhaps even taught to children like a VBS song: "The wise man built his house upon the rock, the wise man. . .") This common story is being assumed by Paul for the sake of his hearers, whom he apparently thinks will be able to track with him.[74]

The parallelism is obvious, and it is easy to perceive how this might flow off the tongue when read aloud to a group. Paul easily adapts this story: *baptized* into Moses; *spiritual* food and drink; *Now, this Rock . . . it was Christ!*

This last phrase is the punch line, and that is how it should be seen—when the smile comes as the chills run up the spine; when the light goes on and you say "Oh wow!" Imagine hearing this story that you already know. "'They used to drink from the following rock.' Yes, yes, we know that." The one reading takes a breath, pauses slightly, and utters a cool but emphatic: *"Now, this Rock . . . it was Christ!"* And so now, all the stories you've ever heard your entire life about water in the desert—how God used to care for his people—they all come to life, rushing toward this one brief comment: *"Now, this Rock; it was Christ!"*[75]

---

[74] There are debates about whether Paul is overshooting his audience, since many were Gentiles, not Jews. Paul did not seem bothered by this.

[75] The view expressed in some commentaries that this phrase is merely a parenthetical note (see discussion in Garland 2003, 458) misses the point entirely. Vv. 4b and 5a are parallel in how they start and end: (4b) *NOW this rock . . . it was CHRIST!* (5a) *NEVERTHELESS not with most of them was pleased GOD!* This was a sharp contrast that could easily be voiced in public reading.

84

English translations tend to flatten the comment, but it deserves better. **First**, the normal word *and* (*kai*) has already been used 6 times in vv. 1-4; and the strong word (*alla*) occurs in v. 5, "*Nevertheless* not with most . . ." So even though the word in 4b (*de*) can often mean either of those, here it is a contrast from the others, like a revelation: "*Now* this Rock . . ." **Second**, although there is nothing spectacular about the word order in 4b, the fact that *Christ* ends this sentence is. It would be normal to say "The rock was *heavy*," where the word heavy would not be emphatic in any way, unless it was placed first: "Now, *heavy* was the rock." In 4b, *rock* might be emphatic because it precedes the Greek verb; but Christ is clearly emphatic, just by virtue of being in such a sentence and being equated with such a thing. Hence *"Now, this Rock; it was Christ!"* is not only defensible, it makes sense. **Third**, aside from all such technicalities, this phrase rolls off the tongue with a certain suspense and surprise, and it comes off that way because they were already part of this ongoing story.

That Craving

Paul continues (in vv. 6-13) masterfully and intricately weaving numerous texts together toward the main subject: a stern warning against craving evil. The internal structure of the Greek sentences shows that this is no ordinary piece, but something that received special attention in writing (see next page).

Glancing at vv. 6-13, it may appear that Paul is just jumping around from one text to another. I've heard people say that about him, that like many preachers today, he wanders in his preaching. 'Taint so. Actually he is quite intricate in the way he selects his texts and in how he brings the whole together. English readers have trouble seeing this because connections and structural features exist on a Greek level.

6	A	a	Now these things became types for our sake,	*Num 11:4, 34*
		b	that we might not go craving after evil	
		c	as some of them craved.	
7	B	a	You are not to become idolaters	*Ex 32:6*
		b	as some of them;	
		c	as it is written,	

> **"The people sat down to eat and drink
> and rose up to play."**

8	C	a	Nor let us practice harlotry,	*Num 25:1*
		b	as some of them practiced harlotry,	
		c	and twenty-three thousand fell in one day.	
9	C	a	Nor let us be tempting Christ,	*Num 21:4-7*
		b	as some of them tempted him	
		c	and were destroyed by asps.	
10	B	a	Nor are you to be grumblers	*Num 11:1*
		b	as some of them grumbled	
		c	and were killed by the destroyer.	
11	A	a	Now these things kept happening to them as types,	*cf. Wisdom 16:2-14*
		b	and they were written for our instruction	
		c	unto whom the end of the ages has come.	

12			So then,
	A		the one who THINKS, "I'm standing!"
		B	Let that one watch so as not to fall!
13		C	No test has overtaken you except what is human.
			D ***And God is faithful!***
		C	He will not permit you to be tested beyond your ability.
		B	Instead, he will also make a way out
	A		with the result that you CAN bear up.

1Cor 10:6-13[76]

Culture of Engagement

Furthermore, Paul's method is at least somewhat similar to ancient synagogue sermons in which the exposition of texts is designed to engage the audience.

1Cor 10:1-13 certainly has homiletic qualities, as though it might have been a stand-alone sermon that Paul or someone else had preached before and Paul is now adapting for this specific context. (What preacher hasn't done that?) Pulling this text out of its current context, it could actually stand alone as a sermon of

---

[76] See Collier 2020, 518, 602 for full description of this layout.

warning to avoid evil craving and to trust in the faithfulness of God to care for his people. If chapter 10 started with v. 14, it would still make sense—just not as much. But whether it was a stand-alone Jewish or Christ-based homily of some type or not, the function of the piece is still sermonic, and it fits this context perfectly. For now, in the context of 1Corinthians 8-11, it is a powerful exposition of texts for the sake of the current faith community.

Even though no specific mention is made of the Corinthian church in 10:1-13, it is clear that its function in context is to warn that the idolatry that exists specifically within the Corinthian church is dangerously undermining its vitality. Here is a general warning in a very specific conversation with the current community, and with very specific outcomes. How can anyone who is accustomed to drinking from Christ himself at the Lord's table even think to keep company with idolatry?

For these reasons, any time spent looking close up at ancient synagogue sermons shows that such sermons were designed to *involve the audience in the process of exposition* (which means there was a synagogue tradition or culture of engagement in such things). For example, in 1971, Joseph Heinemann, looking at early synagogue sermons,[77] noted that there are many public sermons about which

> we do not know very much. [But there is] one pattern which can be clearly recognized as a form created for and used in the live sermon: [the proem—being defined here.] Instead of starting from the first verse of the pericope and expounding it, [the proem-form] begins invariably with a verse taken from elsewhere, mostly from the Haglographa; from this "remote" verse the preacher proceeds to evolve a chain of expositions and interpretations until, at the very end of the proem, he arrives at the first verse of the pericope with which he concludes.[78]

---

[77] These were tannaitic homilies. The Tannaim were the rabbis of the Mishnah (the oral law of the Pharisees written down about 200 CE); the tannaitic period is roughly the first two centuries CE, which of course includes the time of Christ and the birth of Christianity.

[78] Heinemann 1971, esp. 101, 103. After some discussion, Heinemann examines the proem of R. Eleazar b. Azariah on Eccl. xii:11, which he dates it at the end of the first century. This text

On this, I once had a prolonged private conversation[79] with Dr. Lou Silberman, the former Hillel Professor of Jewish Literature and Thought at Vanderbilt. He described ancient synagogue sermons as community events in which the expositor escorted his audience through a series of texts, at first glance unrelated, while keeping his hearers in suspense for how he would resolve the textual tensions. When he finally brought the texts together through exegetical care and skill, the listeners would "Aha!" with delight, being moved from curiosity and suspense to surprise and gratification. It is something just like this that happens in 10:6-13.

The Conversation

So now in 10:6-13 we get to watch Paul enter into a conversation with God and community through a variety of texts and developing traditions. He's not just jumping around quoting or alluding to texts; he is engaging both texts and community! He not only becomes part of the existing textual conversation, he takes his hearers by the hand and leads them along with him. We'll now look at some specifics:

1. His key text is Ex 32:6,[80]
   "They __sat down__ to eat and drink and __rose up__ to play."

2. It tells you exactly what he is about to do. It is the only direct quote in this text. And he is getting ready to use this key to unlock (explain) his *main* text, which is actually Numbers 11.

3. He begins and ends with allusions to Numbers 11. To be more specific, in the Greek OT, Num 11:4 says the people *"sat down"* and 11:34 says the people *"rose up."* In English translations, they don't sit down—they weep. And that is a correct translation of the Hebrew text. But in Greek, they

concludes with an exhortation (114-116). There are obvious similarities between what Heinemann describes and 1Cor 10:1-13, at least in broad terms, even if there are also differences in detail. It would be too much to claim that 1Cor 10:1-13 is an early proem. Yet, it is not too much to suggest (based on Heinemann) that 1Cor 10:1-13 exhibits traits of later established homiletic forms. It is at least possible that it originated as an independent homily on Numbers 11. For the depth of midrashic/homiletic manner in 1Cor 10:1-13, see Collier 1994.

[79] A private conversation with Lou Silberman at a week-long seminar on the Dead Sea Scrolls, at Ghost Ranch Education and Retreat Center, New Mexico, 1991.

[80] I developed this case in great detail in Collier 1994.

don't weep; they make camp and dwell there. And this is exactly the same word that is used to say that someone sits down. So, in Numbers 11 Greek text, they *sit down* and they *rise up*. And what they do between 11:4 and 34 is tragic. They crave meat to the point that Yahweh's anger is described as "blazing hotly!"

4. When Paul directly quotes Ex 32:6, he is conversing not only with the words *sat down* and *rose up*, but with what it means to play; i.e., to play the harlot. To sell out. That's what happened in the bulk of Numbers 11.

5. Once he quotes the key text, Ex 32:6, he walks backwards through Numbers (from 25:1 to 21:4-7 to 11:1 finally back to verse 1!) pulling together *food texts* that are now strung together midrashically[81] on the phrase found in Ex 32:6—they *sat down and they rose up to play*. All of these food texts show Israel being led into harlotry, testing Christ, and grumbling.

Throughout this text, Paul is weaving together allusions to these texts and, by extension, to others like them: Pss 78, 106; Num 14:16; Num 11:4, 34; Ex 32:6; Num 25:1; 21:4-7; 11:1; cf. Wisdom 16:2-14; and still others.[82] He is also very clearly speaking from within popular understandings found only in the larger community conversation (a "following" rock—not in any OT text). Paul is not doing this "off the cuff," he is speaking a known language.

The problem, here, explaining 1Cor 10:1-13 in the manner I just have, is like watching the entire race of the Indianapolis 500 speeded up into two minutes. It is not enough, really, to simply

---

[81] I have kept repeating the definition of this word *midrash* through the book, since I know that for some of my readers it will be a completely new term. First, in chapter 1, I showed that Paul is utilizing ancient Jewish methods of interpretation that are similar to later rabbis and were based in biblical texts. Although a highly controversial term among biblical scholars, I have argued that the term מדרש|*midrash* from the start (1) was associated with the telling and/or retelling of a distinctively Jewish story: a YHWH Story; and (2) was concerned with how that YHWH story functioned as an ongoing "deliverance" story. See Collier 2020, 603; and also the entirety of chapter 9. In the present book see also p. 39.

[82] There is a lot of scholarly controversy over exactly which texts Paul was alluding to, and I address this in Collier 1994. The case I've made does not suggest that no other texts would apply—they would *all* apply and feed the story (pun intended)! There are specific links that have Paul referring to specific texts, as I have listed.

hear about this, or to think the point can be "got" just by such a fast run-through, or to think that this alone qualifies one to drive in the race. The complexity and "interwovenness" of all of these stories only becomes visible and fathomable once we allow ourselves to become part of the conversation.[83]

So What?

In this place, Paul does not merely "quote" or "use" or "read" or "encounter" or "accidentally bump into" these texts. He *interacts with* and *engages* them; he is *in conversation with* them from within a long-lived community of discussion. Markus Bockmuehl is spot on when he notes that NT writers

> speak as they do because they are *thunderstruck* by the pressure that Scripture . . . exerts on their own view of things."[84]

This is clearly the language of *engagement* and is exactly on point. All of this fits 1Corinthians 8-11 perfectly. The end of the piece, 10:12-13, is a delight to the eyes and ears, and we all proclaim, "Aha!" *God is **faithful!*** Who in their right mind could walk away from this now to crave meat at an idol's temple?

This is all a perfect example of a protracted Shade 3 conversation. It is not a normal interchange between two people (S1), and it is not prayer (S2). Here is a biblical author engaging deeply in an already-existing, centuries-old conversation coming down from both ancient texts and tradition (S3). And they all were asking: "How is God working in the world today?"

---

[83] As with Collier 1994
[84] As quoted from a personal letter in Hays 2014, x. Repeated in Hays 2016a.

PART 3:
TRANSFORMATION

In molecular biology and genetics,
transformation
is the genetic alteration of a cell resulting from
the direct incorporation through the cell membrane(s)
of DNA originating from outside its surroundings.
(from Wikipedia, "Transformation [genetics]")

Stated otherwise
for our purposes here,
in simple terms . . .

In the reading of biblical texts,
transformation
*is how we stop **simply reading** the Bible*
*and start having **ongoing Conversation***
with biblical texts and their authors
*—**with God himself!**—*
by seeing and doing things we've never done before!

Action 1
Preparation

To begin such a conversation,
we must prepare in and for ourselves
a mindset, an expectation, and a physical space
—as if we are getting ready for a visit
from a close friend or small group!

_9_

Your Mindset

You got up late this morning after texting too long last night with your best friend about some random issue. Consequently, the kids and the dog were acting up this morning. Traffic was heavy and you spilled your coffee. You arrive at your interview five minutes late. "Sorry, sorry!" You feel flustered. You smile nervously. You have trouble answering questions about why you left your previous job. After an unusually short time, the interviewer thanks you and says she'll let you know.

Creation as Preparation

The fact that some people actually go to job interviews like this is truly a dumbfounding thing. But they do! Anybody can have a bad day; but being unprepared for such a meeting is a different issue. No *self-respecting* person would ever go to a job interview completely unprepared like this—especially not for a high-level career move or a job that is worth anything. Most of us would move heaven and earth to *create for and in ourselves* the right *mindset*, the right *expectation*, and the right *spaces* needed to help us put our best foot forward—not just to *look* our best, but to *be* our best self.

And *create* is the right word! We would *make* it happen! We would make sure we carved out the time we needed; get people out of our hair; wear the right shirt, tie, suit, or dress; spend mirror time smiling and practicing question-and-answer; review our personal information to eliminate all mistakes; and think seriously about how to state clearly what we "plan to bring to this amazing organization"—as well as what we hope to find from it. We might not fret or worry over it. But we would certainly not think of going into such a meeting unprepared.

And then there's the Bible: "the most important book in the history of the world"— we say. The most important interview we will ever have. How do we prepare for it? Sometimes, Christians won't even lift a finger to get ready for it. It's the Bible! It's supposed to be easy!

How do we create a mindset worthy of entering into conversation with biblical texts and authors?

Some will immediately say "Prayer!" And of course prayer is vital. But prayer is a launching pad, not a hiding place, so let's get even more disciplined and specific in our thinking: *How do we go from **watching** Paul (or any other biblical writer) to actually **engaging** him in conversation? How do we stop being an outsider looking in, and actually join in the conversation?*

Do we simply mimic Paul or other biblical writers?

The answer is "NO!" We do not simply mimic anyone!

Christians need to become clear about this: *It is not our goal to duplicate Paul's or anyone else's culture or cultural methods.* That is a huge mistake. It would be like dressing ourselves in the same garb as the Italian astronomer, Galileo Galilei, in hopes that we, too, might make great scientific discoveries. If that is our goal, we would do better to study his ideas, and then study science since that time, and then do our own thinking. Playing "dress-up" won't really do much for us—except at a costume party.

Creating a Mindset

To create a mindset for *Biblical Conversation*, there are some key principles that we need to learn.

1. Avoid the "Straight Line" Fallacy

When it comes to interpretive procedure, there is no straight line from any biblical writer to our time and place.[85] So when asking, *"What do we do now?"* our focus should turn more to their intense desire for conversation with God for the sake of the living community than on any odd cultural trappings it might come in. Just dressing ourselves up like them won't do us any good.

For example, we might learn a great deal from how some ancient writers (in OT and NT texts) understood God was acting in the world, or how they wrestled with the problem of evil, or suffering, or war, or slavery, or racism, or sexism. We also might learn from how some other writers (in both OT and NT) wrestled with and *adjusted* some of those ideas. We will learn a great deal from all of that; but we do not want to become polly parrots simply blurting out sacred, set-in-stone positions.

Now we certainly may have direct access to God through Jesus for salvation or for help and comfort, but it is a fallacy to think that there is some kind of imaginary straight line from Isaiah, Paul, or even Jesus that will make us read biblical texts exactly like they did.[86] Such a view never considers the vital role of a faith community that is always *in conversation* about such things.

When reading the Bible, we should realize that we are being invited to enter thoughtfully and with great energy into the conversation *as participants*—never as robots. But some faith circles focus more on top-down reading—"God said it, so we do it!" Obedience is a good thing—of course it is!—but within a context where *we pay close attention to the intensity of those*

---

[85] This was addressed in the first five chapters without using this terminology.
[86] Collier 1993 talks about reading the Bible like Jesus, but it soon becomes obvious that this is not any kind of "straight-line" formula.

ancient conversations, and then resolve to become participants ourselves, thinking alongside our brothers and sisters from generations past. And now we bring the best that we ourselves have to bring.

For example, let us name a few *molten-hot topics*: how biblical writers did or did not address things like marriage and divorce, or the relation and role of women and men, or sexual mores, or racism, or sexism. I specifically mention such things because on such things we really get to see whether we are more interested in reading carefully or in preserving already-believed stuff. These are such touchy subjects, that just with the comment I made just now, someone reading this just now has already said: "Aha! *There* is this guy's motive for writing this book! *I knew it!*" Actually, this kind of reaction might show the *reader's* motive more than my own. My motive is to talk about the importance and necessity of real, honest, and genuine conversation, regardless of beliefs or prejudices we may already have. The big question we should be asking is this: "*How is God working through his people today?*" The simplistic answer (that he never changes[87]) dodges the necessity of thoughtful interaction and encourages the decomposition of real community.

If we can't have genuine conversation about things like this without everybody getting mad and drawing lines, then the idea of a "faith community" is a sad joke and a sham that we are trying to foist onto the world as if it came from God.

Now let's take a different example—a *non*-rabble-rousing example: *ancient interpretive practices*. Few people know about this topic, let alone do they care about it. But from it, we can observe and track the motivations, concerns, and practices of our ancient bothers and sisters. That does not mean we should copy-

---

[87] Based on a complete misreading of Heb 13:8, by mixing it with overarching and simplistic and ill-formed doctrines (and popular Christian songs) about God being unchangeable. Coincidentally, the KJV uses the word *conversation* twice in Hebrews 13, but this is based on a now obsolete meaning of the word as "conduct or behavior." So it has nothing to do with the question at hand. The KJV uses this translation 20 times for a handful of Hebrew and Greek words that generally mean "way of life." Ps 37:14; 50:23; 2Cor 1:12; Gal 1:13; Eph 2:3; 4:22; Phil 1:27; 3:20; 1Tim 4:12; Heb 13:5, 7; Jas 3:13; 1Pet 1:15, 18; 2:12; 3:1, 2, 16; 2Pet 2:7; 3:11.

cat their cultural methods. We live in a very different time with very different cultural mores, expectations, thought processes, and goals. They had the courage to tackle such things. We honor them when we bring our best to do the same. There is no straight line.

2. Keep it Simple

Especially starting out, it is a good idea to aim at light conversation. Just like in everyday interactions, it is always possible to come back later for more. No one is trying to turn you into some kind of biblical scholar. This really should not be all that difficult for anyone who actually wants to have genuine conversations with biblical authors. If you start simple and keep it that way for awhile, you will do a better job of understanding and mastering the principles of good *Biblical Conversation* skills. Once you have those down, you can strengthen them to any deeper level you like.

3. "I-FACE" the Bible

Worthwhile, personal, face-to-face conversations don't just happen all by themselves. Effective conversations require that we pay attention to some important factors.[88] The following five are a crucial minimum: Both parties must

1. be truly *in-the-moment,*

2. bring *focus,*

3. practice the *art of listening* (before we open our own big mouth to start speaking),

4. show genuine *care* and *concern* for the other party, and

5. *energetically participate* in the conversation (as if we *want* to be in it).

---

[88] There are countless articles, books, school programs, seminars, and classes on what makes for effective conversation. It is not a "fluff" topic.

We could expand the list; but at least these are essential. Take any one of these out (stop focusing or showing concern, for example), and the interchange suffers.

It may help to remember these characteristics by reading them poetically as a *chiasm* (where the item at the center is usually most important, and the flanking items tend to correlate):

a <u>I</u>n the Moment
   b <u>F</u>ocus
      c <u>A</u>rt of Listening
   b <u>C</u>are
a <u>E</u>nergy

The *Art of Listening* certainly does belong at the center of any worthwhile conversation, and being *in the moment* with *energy*, and *focusing* with great *care* and *concern* will aid in that listening process. Good listening is active listening, where the hearer is asking questions to clarify and understand.

We all know what it's like to be in a conversation with someone who keeps checking his "smart phone," or who keeps interrupting to say her piece and then won't shut up, or who is just plain not paying attention. That is not a conversation; it is a waste of time!

"I-FACE" can genuinely help. If we were to memorize this and then practice it in every conversation we have, it would change our world; and it would help to transform *reading* the Bible into *conversing* with it.

First, these are obviously not "methods for reading" or "steps" to take, one after the other; instead, they show *which way we are leaning* when we read. We all can easily recognize which way people are leaning when they stomp their way into a room with a scowl, as opposed to whistling a happy tune. How we are leaning when we open a Bible makes a difference. If you say to yourself, "I-FACE the Bible!" and recall the acronym, it can help you *lean toward becoming a participant* (instead of leaning away from it).

4. Understand The Golden Arch

Leaning-in, we now need to understanding how three elements interrelate. It is not just that there are three points (hence, it's not a triangle); it is the manner and order in which these interact.

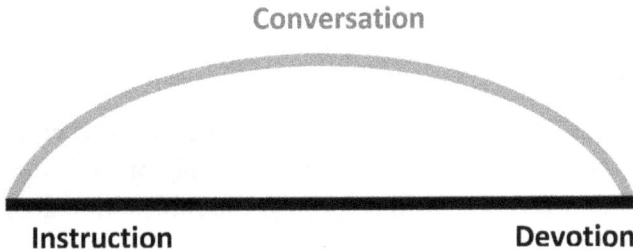

Conversation

Instruction   **Devotion**

Figure 4: Golden Arch

We've seen *instruction* and *devotion* in chapters 4-5, in the *disciplines for the text and the self.* In order to go from concerns about the text (**instruction**) to concerns about God in our lives (**devotion**), or vice versa, we now will intentionally and imaginatively engage in **conversation** *with* and *about* both. It is this conversation that allows us to understand both and bridge them, as if sitting down with the author over coffee.

5. Make It Real

The notion of *Biblical Conversation* is new for many people, so it is a challenging idea that seems strange. But it is not a metaphorical or theoretical step; it is *an actual, verbal conversation that takes place, in many cases, out loud.* It involves actually sitting down with a cup of coffee, hot chocolate, tea (or whatever you want to drink) and visualizing the author sitting with you. It takes a little getting used to; but it is a warm skill that anyone can learn. It is part science, art, and habit—and part allowing yourself to do something a little different, maybe even outside of your current comfort zone, all for the sake of growing; and it asks you to open your *imagination.* Like any skill, this one comes with a learning curve; but once learned, it can have a powerful impact on how we experience the Bible.

If we have a mindset already against such things, we cannot possibly engage in it. The five things mentioned here can help re-orient the way we think about having coffee with Paul (or any other biblical author). It helps us get ready to become participants.

Breakthrough

All of this comes with a promise. If you commit yourself to these things, you will experience an incredible breakthrough to a new level of awareness with respect to the Bible. Some lights will start to go on.

Our test groups in the *Institute for the Art of Biblical Conversation (IABC)* show that this approach is extremely powerful—even with people who initially resist it (and who say "I've never read that way before!"). We've been testing and developing this since 2012 and it turns out to be a wonderfully alluring approach for helping people engage with the biblical text and with each other on levels that many have never before experienced.

Here's what three different people in our group have said about this approach when I asked, "what can we do to improve this?"

#1: This approach has spoiled me for all other Bible studies!

#2: These conversations with Paul opened up a whole new way of viewing scripture and it changed how I study the Bible.

#3: [This conversational approach] is of such high caliber, and is so compelling, and speaks so directly to my life that I have a hard time putting it down and getting on with my day.... I don't know what you can do to make things better, but I do know this— DON'T DUMB IT DOWN!

In our online development and test group, we are proposing that Christian readers of the Bible learn how to have a cup of coffee with a biblical author while having a substantive and real conversation with that author through his text—as if sitting across the table. In our group, we started with one of the earliest documents of the NT to have been written (1Thessalonians). The class response was (to use one of Paul's Greek words in that letter) *huper-ek-peris-sou!—quite beyond all measure!*[89]

Since 2012, we have developed the conversational approach in cooperation with hundreds of people testing the material, gathering feedback, and making adjustments. Our experience has been a feeling of something nothing short of a breakthrough!

Clearly, there is more to this than just drinking coffee while reading the Bible! Lot's of people do that already! Furthermore, one does not need to be part of our group or any other group to adopt the general *principles* stated above and the *practices* that are coming below.

Creating a *mindset* that will allow for conversation is a crucial step! But we still need to talk about creating *genuine expectation*.

---

[89] 1Th 3:10; 5:13. See Collier 2020, 554: "Here is the highest form of comparison imaginable (BDAG 1033a). This wording, in context, reveals the nature of Paul's elation, emotion, and exuberance. Night and day indicates the never-ending nature of his request."

_10_

Your Expectation

It is mouthwatering when we take with us through a day a healthy, vibrant, eager expectation for the good that is about to happen next. It dramatically affects how we experience everything.[90] When we strive for something good, there is everything right and proper with holding a vision of hope between us and what we may actually be facing.

This is especially true when reading the Bible. When we approach it with an *open and energetic expectation* of what could possibly happen from a forthcoming conversation[91] with its authors and texts—truly remarkable things can come of this. It might not be a miracle, but it can certainly feel miraculous.

How do we create and nurture such positive, forward-looking, healthy expectations when it comes to having conversations with biblical authors and texts? How do we keep away from unrealistic expectations and focus on the healthy ones?

---

[90] I'm not talking about "magical thinking" here—the *unrealistic expectations* that set us up for disappointment and failure. There is also such a thing as *oppressive expectation* (sometimes called "premeditated regrets") where we expect others to act a certain way or live up to what we think they should do or be. These are quite unhealthy and not the point here at all. See Johnson 2018.

[91] See p. 98 fn. 86 for comments about the KJV on *conversation*.

Create and Nurture

After years of experience with this, and with hundreds of people, I suggest that there are seven down-to-earth, realistic, but essential, key actions that we can take.

These work!

1. *Believe* that you can have a conversation

It starts here. If you don't believe it is even *possible*, then it can't happen.

You have to be able to take the word *conversation* at face value, that a conversation between you and that text is a viable thing. You ask questions (as in any conversation), and this drives you back into it, to listen to it, and to find answers or even more questions. So, for example, you might ask: "Hey, Paul, why did you say the word 'election' here in 1Th 1:4?" And then you go back to the text to hear how Paul might answer that and challenge you.

Asking these kinds of questions is not easy, especially at first. However, this is how you participate in the conversation from beginning to end through sight, sound, imagination, and touch, as in any one-on-one personal conversation. *But first, you have to believe it is possible—even if you don't know how to do it.*

2. *Engage* your imagination energetically

Yes, your *imagination* is a vital part of this. You have to be willing to light it up! This is not usually encouraged when speaking about the Bible; in fact, it is often *dis*couraged. Not so here. Indeed, the more you can imagine yourself actually sitting across the table one-on-one with the biblical author you are talking with, the more valuable your experience will be.[92]

---

[92] This is not about silly questions, like "Hey Paul what color is your hat?" Or about making up ideas wholesale. This is about questions appropriate to the text at hand, not about creating some fantastic fiction. It's about allowing your imagination to push, lead, or guide you back into the text.

If you will learn to do this, it will literally begin a process of waking up your sensors, and it will enhance your conversational experience. You will be talking with these authors[93] about letters or documents they once wrote a long time ago; but eventually you will get around to talking about the life you are now living. Look at this as a dialogue between you and those authors—as a real, personal conversation.

Now, in what follows, I'm going to say "Paul" a lot here so that I don't have to keep referring to a nameless author. But this can apply to every biblical document, even if it is written anonymously. Just imagine an author who is implied by and consistent with the text.

So then, if you can imagine that *Paul has somehow entered into your time and place* and that he is conversant with the issues you face, you will increase your ability to make a real connection. This is not about dismissing Paul's ancient context; it is a way of making sense of it. Together you will speak of God and life. He will tell you what it was like for him to live, work, and write at the time he did, but he will do it in a way that will help you live in yours.

If you can *imagine* that Paul is wanting to hear from *you*, that he is asking *you* to respond to what he says, you will then go a long way to realizing that "reading the Bible" is never a one-way street.

Paul is not lecturing or merely talking to hear himself speak; he wants to hear from you. *He needs a conversation partner just like you.* In fact, his letters were written for that very purpose! In the book *"I, Paulos"* (347ff) I specifically make the case that 1Thessalonians is intended, above all, as a letter of *intimate apostolic conversation.*

---

[93] While we are on this topic, of a personal conversation, is it possible that any of these authors were women? I use the pronoun *he* for biblical authors as a convenience since it is likely *technically* correct. However, *technically* is a key word for the *completed* books. No one should think that one or more women did not have significant influence over or input into what is in biblical texts such as Ruth or the stories in the Gospels (especially the Gospel of John). Even the very story of the empty tomb itself is the story by women. Even the Gospels give them that credit. We should never imagine that the voice of women in our texts was not significant. This is another way of remembering that our texts resulted from the outpouring of *community* conversation.

Naturally, all of this conversing and listening and imagining is about getting closer to God. This is not about confusing Paul or any other author with God. But conversing with that one who emerges from the text you are reading is a key part of understanding what led him to write what he wrote in pursuit of God—even in collaboration with the larger community, women and men alike.

Imagination is a key to effective *Biblical Conversation*, not for the sake of fantasy, but for engagement. It is reading with the mind, but also with the heart and soul.

3. *Think* about how a conversation might look.

The point is to visualize yourself in an actual conversation with a biblical author. See it in your mind. Maybe you invite one author, maybe a group that influence him. Maybe you are reading the Gospel of John and you have Mary Magdalene at your table, along with the author, and you get to ask her, "How did you influence the writing of these stories to help others believe? And to the author, "When telling this story, what was it like being able to hear some of this from others who were there?" This kind of personal involvement will spark other creative juices that will help you stay interested.

4. *Embrace* speaking in the first person

You must do this if you want to make this more real, current, and urgent. You imagine Paul, James, Matthew, Isaiah (whomever) at your table speaking to you in the first person—and you to them. Speak to them as you would to anyone else.

Now don't get hung up on the pitfalls, like "But I don't know that much (or anything) about this author!" That doesn't matter. It might even be better. Don't look up *anything* about the author, just let the document you are reading provide whatever information it provides. Let it be a world of its own. Draw your conclusions about the author from the text in front of you. What does *it* tell you about the author?

For example, even if we know nothing about Paul as a person from any other source, we can honestly talk to Paul like this:

Hey Paul, we can tell just by reading 1Thessalonians how passionate you are about your calling for the Gospel message. You are obviously even willing to die for it! We are also touched deeply by how tremendously tender you are toward your dear friends in this letter. You are profoundly concerned that they stand firm in that message, and you go to incredible lengths to help them understand what's at stake, and to offer them great hope. We wondered if you might be an old softy, just saying nice things about everyone—but you are actually quite willing to say some very harsh things about your enemies! Wow! (You would get into all kinds of trouble today for that!) And, oh my, we began to notice just how much time you have spent yourself conversing with our sacred authors—the same ones that are in our Bible today! It is so interesting and touching to watch how their ideas now ooze from your normal speech. How impressive and marvelous this is as a model for us![94]

We can tell all of this (and a whole lot more) just by speaking to Paul in the first person while reading this one letter!

5. *Decide to always keep things in context.*

Keeping texts in context is what makes actual conversation possible. Otherwise, you can wander off into rambling speculation.

"Contextual conversation" is a key principle for all successful interaction. Do you like it when others take your words out of context? Then don't do that to other people; and don't do it biblical authors! They wouldn't appreciate it any more than you do. So, instead of playing hop-scotch all over the Bible like so many people do—Ouija board style—to find proof-texts or devotionally compatible tidbits, don't do that! Walk through

---

[94] This is not a quote from anywhere; it is a first person retelling drawn entirely from 1Thessalonians in a kind of summary fashion. As for "conversing with sacred authors" in 1Thessalonians, commentators far too easily pass over this in this letter, making sweeping comments like "no OT reference here." This is misleading. See Collier 2020, 574-89 for a summary.

whatever document you are having the conversation with one contextual step at a time—just like in a respectful conversation. Contextual conversation applies both to responsible listening (to the author's or original readers' context) and responsible application to your own life (*your* context).

6. *Focus* on how you will be stretched and inspired to grow.

If you know in your heart that you are going to benefit, this will inspire you to keep going, even when you feel you are not quite sure what you are doing. Think about how you are going to be stretched. What do you stand to gain? How will this help you in reading the Bible? How will it affect your understanding? What could happen to bring you into a closer relationship with God? What could allow you to put down roots of faith into biblical soil to help you hold on when the winds start blowing? Create a stable, reliable, motivated expectation within yourself by focusing on how you might be growing.

7. *Allow* yourself to process each experience.

This will help create even more interest in the approach. Allow yourself to *process* your progress. Pay attention to your experiences as you move through every conversation. Embrace your past successes as well as the successful experience of others. How you *process* your experiences is how you drink it in and relate it to all the parts of your *self* (as spoken of in chapter 5). This is where personal transformation occurs.

Breakthrough

These seven key actions will help you create and sustain a steady expectation—and yet one that will keep you on the edge of your seat—for what can happen for you if you will simply commit to starting up conversations with biblical authors and texts.

Naturally, there are always the naysayers who will object to every single one of these. They will say things like, *"I don't like pipe dreams; I like to be realistic!"* But once again, in the words of the wise old Yoda: *"That is why you fail!"* And in the words of the teacher of all teachers, Jesus: *"If you have faith the size of a grain of mustard seed, you can move mountains."* And again: *"If you put your hands to the plow only to look back with a longing for the good ol' things, you are going to be plowing very crooked rows!"* Yes, these occur in specific contexts; but they also are macro principles that speak to human potential and human nature.

To any who seek (even a shred of) adventure or have (even an ounce of) faith, these can incredibly impact the way your see and experience the Bible. They will help you create and build wonderful, healthy, excited expectation for learning to read conversationally!

11

Your Private Space

The family is gathered, the turkey is baked, the stuffing is stuffed—it's time to eat! But wait! We have no dining room, no table, no chairs, no plates, no spoons or forks or knives. Can we still eat? Well, it's possible. But it will be a very different kind of experience.

Trying to have a conversation with biblical authors while keeping it purely imaginary is equally fraught with problems. A physical space properly set up can help you create a conversational atmosphere that not only is conducive to conversation, the space can actually *invite it!*

To get ready for a conversation with biblical authors, there are some physical things we should do. And these are not just "things to do." This involves a little bit of creative thinking and a desire to put yourself into the best possible place for ongoing conversational experiences. This does not have to be elaborate, expensive, or time consuming. Simple is good. Even so, this can grow over time.

Set up Your "Conversation Area"

1. Create a "Conversation Area."

If possible, make a space dedicated for this very purpose: a desk, a couple of chairs, a table, or even a whole room. Let this become your *closet* Jesus speaks about when he says, "when thou prayest, *enter into thy closet . . .*" (Mt 6:6 KJV).[95] This isn't a clothes closet, but a *tameion, a* private room where one can be alone. Large or small is no matter. It's a place for privacy. Joseph, overcome by seeing his brother Benjamin, quickly withdrew to a *private room* to weep (Gen 43:30). Proverbs uses this same word to speak of one's "innermost being" (Prov 26:22). Make this a place that is, for you, conducive for actual, private, focused conversation—just like you would sit with a close friend.

a. It can be large or small, cozy or spartan, fancy or plain— whatever appeals to you.

b. If possible, you should make this a place that is *dedicated* to this purpose. Make it so that when you come to this area, it almost *calls* you to sit down for another go.

2. Stock your area.

You should have access close by to multiple Bibles and any study books you already have or might acquire. Ideally, you'll have a computer with Bible software, but this is not essential. You might start out with only a few of these things, but it can grow over time.

This is not just you and a Bible and book of devotions! This is you creating a space for conversation with biblical authors. For that, you need more versatility.

---

[95] This has been discussed for many years in many contexts. The movie "The War Room" (2015) focuses on the importance of such a room. But I am after something that goes beyond such discussions. These primarily focus only on prayer or prayer with devotional Bible reading methods. Very powerful and important things. But for Shade 3 conversations to take place, a different kind of emphasis has to be understood.

By all means, you should use several English translations along with your own Bible. Some people fight this. "I like my own Bible!" Or "I don't like all these newfangled translations!" Or "One is enough!" Nobody is trying to replace your Bible. As a matter of fact, you should keep your main Bible handy and use it all the time. But learn the value of using a variety of English translations to your benefit. Use the translations together to give you a broader sense of the text.

3. Get something to drink!

Now get a cup of coffee, tea, hot chocolate, or other drink and sit in that space. The point of this is for you to be comfortable and focused, and for you to associate this experience with other physical stimuli. Creating such a warm environment can greatly increase your joy of the moment. You will find that, after a short time of doing this, your space, on its own, will begin calling out to you.

Establish How You Will Proceed

1. Resolve to stay focused.

Decide you are going to use this area as a focused place for conversation. You could even make it a holy place, dedicated solely to that purpose. But even if it needs to be a multipurpose area, don't waste time on Facebook or Twitter here, or other such activities that destroy critical thinking ability. Decide to stay on target.

2. Keep a schedule.

Five days a week is ideal. Make a pact with yourself to set aside at least 15-30 minutes a day for 5 days. Then take a couple of days off. You know your own schedule and personal preferences, but daily tends to work best. Also, *set aside a routine time of day* for each session (if you can), whether morning, afternoon, or evening. Frankly, whether you come to a session every day, week, or other interval is up to you, but try to approach it with some consistency. The more consistent, the better.

Keep a schedule, but be flexible. Consider adding more time on one or more of the five days. Especially for days three and four, set aside an additional 15-30 minutes for those days—if you can. It is up to you, but this kind of self-discipline is helpful for developing a healthy reading life.

One more thing. You can't just do this once or twice and expect it to work. Try it for at least 21 days and then evaluate it. Our experience on this with all kinds of groups and individuals (regardless of age, gender, or educational background). Those who start and stay with it develop a love for it. This is a powerful activity that can help you engage in the process personally.

3. Stoke your imagination.

Actively and purposely imagine that you are spending personal time with that biblical author. No, this is not silly. This right here causes some people to stand up from the table and walk away. Honestly, because they have never done such a thing or are not accustomed to it, some get almost defiant over this! No one can make you do this. It has to be voluntary. But if this activity could change your Bible reading life for the better, wouldn't it be worth some effort on your part to give it a fair shot?

4. Take one lesson at a time.

If you try to do everything at once, you'll soon burn out. Always take one session or lesson, and only one, at a time. Our printed material is designed specifically for this, but if you are working on your own, you need to pace yourself. It really doesn't work if you speed read your Bible to get it over with. You can do it, but you'll miss the most important part.

This is about developing a relationship with God through processing what you read during each conversation, as if in conversation with Paul. The *process* is part of what makes the approach unique and what brings power to it. Since it is cumulative, pacing helps.

Engage

Actually use your space! Engage in the process. To get you started, Part IV will provide easy-to-follow, step-by-step procedures for a day by day approach.

Action 2
Conversation

Now, finally, like Jacob wrestling God,
we proclaim,
"I won't let go till you bless me!"
We turn directly to
how to engage in Biblical Conversation.

What follows is a step-by-step approach
that transforms our Bible reading
into an artful, exhilarating
conversation.

PROBE Template Guides
are found in
Appendix A.

−12−

PROBE Basic

You and a friend take a winter outing together up in the mountains. After a long drive, you trudge through the snow to your cabin, unpack your bags, build a fire, and sit down to enjoy it. But your friend pulls out a smartphone and begins doing who knows what. You ask a question or two, and your friend looks up and smiles with a quick answer, and then dives right back into the phone. When you say, "I was hoping we could talk some," your friend replies, "Oh, yeah, let's do that. I can hear everything you say! Go ahead!" And then goes back to the phone. You try a few comments and a question or two, but you increasingly feel like you are in the room by yourself.

After three days of this, you are returning home in the car, when your friend says, "Seems like we just got here, but we didn't get much chance to talk!" That's when you slam on your brakes and try to throw your friend out of the front windshield. (Well, maybe not actually.)

No friend who respects you would ever do this, of course. But this is exactly how way too many people approach the Bible: undisciplined, haphazard, unfocused, not really present, and certainly not prepared. We are too often like one who says to the Bible in front of us, "You go ahead, I can hear every word you say!"

Biblical conversation is like any other personal conversation. You have to be present with it, be serious about it, and want to engage in it.

You start by saying, *"I-FACE this text!"*[96] You bring healthy expectations to the process.[97] And you are set and ready to go.[98]

Overview

PROBE offers an easy-to-learn, step-by-step path into breathtaking moments of conversations with biblical authors through their texts. Here, you engage biblical authors in responsible, contextual, and life-altering interactions; awareness is heightened, aptitude is increased, skills are honed. PROBE has two levels: Basic and Prime. Prime is merely Basic scaled up. Once you've learned Basic, you'll understand Prime.

A Promise

You must *want* the personal growth that PROBE Basic offers. You must want it enough that you will *decide* going in to stay with the process long enough to allow it to take effect. You will be learning new skills; nobody learns new skills for the fun of it! (We do the work of learning skills so we can get the benefits. Skills take a little time to develop. They are often not fun.)

So here is a promise: If you will stay focused on your growth goals (*what you want*) and commit to the PROBE Basic process, giving your best effort, you will begin to see results usually by the end of the first week—*at the very latest* by the end of the second week. God will bless your effort! However, if you only try this one or two days and then quit, *nothing* is going to happen for you. As with anything of value, half-hearted attempts will fail, and they usually fail fast.

---

[96] Chapter 9.
[97] Chapter 10.
[98] Chapter 11.

This needs to be on the table from the very start: *This conversational approach is for people who **earnestly** want more from the Bible.* They are energetic about it and take it seriously in their lives. They see the potential, they sense the value, and they are willing to walk the needed path to experience the kind of growth that God promises to grant.

Through God's grace, PROBE will challenge you to *bring* your best, and it promises to *bring out* your best.

A Portrait

So what does it look like? PROBE is an acronym for a direct, easy-to-follow, 5-day study cycle—always in the order given— where all 5 steps are on a single block of text that you read every day with different agendas. In effect, this is a layered, 5-step approach that brings engaged listening and question-asking to the forefront.

You take one step at a time. This will work if you are a complete novice, never having read the Bible before, or if you have been reading the Bible for years. Either way, it will call out the best you have to bring. And God will bless.

Here is a portrait of the PROBE Basic process.

Biblical Text

P	R	O	B	E
Pre-Read	Recap	Observe	Brainstorm	Engage
Day 1	Day 2	Day 3	Day 4	Day 5

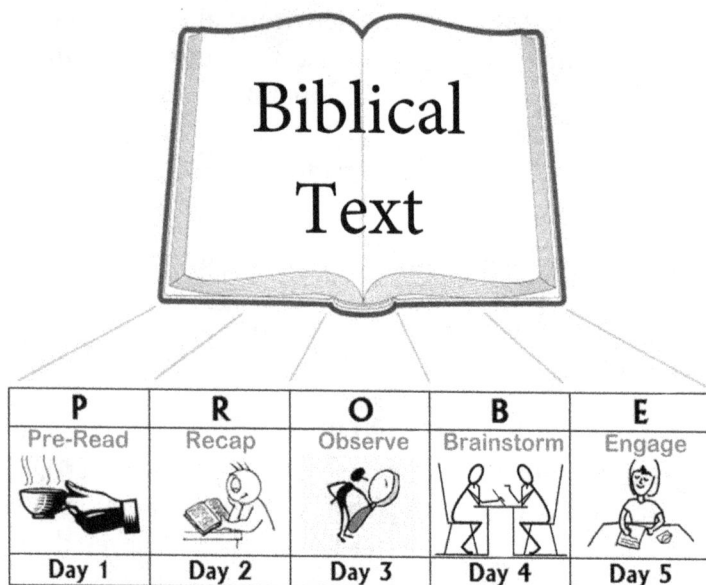

Figure 5: PROBE

Day

1. **Pre-Read**: Read through the block of text itself in at least two English translations.

2. **Recap**: Read it again in new translation. Write a summary of what this text is about. (Can combine this with 1.)

3. **Observe**: Read it again. Look at details. Take specific textual notes. Mark context, key words & phrases. Do word studies. (Can spend 2 days here.)

4. **Brainstorm**: Read it again. *W/author:* Ask questions about what he is doing & read for answers. *W/others:* Study Bibles, Commentaries, Teachers, Friends. (Or spend 2 days here.)

5. **Engage:** Read it again. Tell the author what you learned. Ask author your main question for the week. What does this text help you (a) think or decide? (b) do? (c) What would author say to you or your church now?

A Practice

Here are four notes about how PROBE Basic can be put into practice. The fourth note points to the *PROBE Template Guides* which are found in Appendix A.

1. Can Use Daily

This works well for *daily* interaction. Each morning or evening, 5 days each week, you would (ideally) take your drink with you into your space for 15 to 30 minutes and create for yourself a regular, focused conversation time with your chosen biblical author. You can use the *PROBE Template Guides* for each day (see Appendix A).

For example, let's say that you have decided to read 1Thessalonians at only about 5-8 verses at a time. Each day of the week (M-F) you would read directly from the biblical text in a different translation, and you would have slightly different activities each day, one day building upon the day before. On **Monday through Wednesday** you would read the biblical text for yourself and do what each step says to do. Only on **Thursday** would you look at any commentaries or other helps. On **Friday**, you would focus on application.

This kind of daily repetition can take hold in a way that you might not expect. Obviously, you don't have to start on Monday; it's set up to be flexible. Once you get familiar with the procedure and see the logic and intuition of it, you might want to combine **P-R**-O-B-E, and then spend two sessions on either **O** or **B**. It's flexible.

2. Can Fit to Your Own Schedule

But maybe a daily routine is not right or best for you. Don't feel forced into something you can't do. Maybe you prefer 3 days a week, or some other practice that fits your timetable. You would still use the *PROBE Template Guides* for each day you decide to meet (see Appendix A). You could simply decide to spend an hour or so three days a week, or maybe just not worry about finishing in a week. In this case, you would let every 5-step cycle complete itself on its own schedule. You'd still follow the path, however.

For deeper, more involved study projects, you would move into PROBE Prime (chapter 13). But it's the exact same structure. Starting with Basic keeps it simple.

Just one thing: *Whether you are following Basic or Prime, leave the **order of the sessions** exactly like they are currently set up.* These sessions are specifically layered—one on top the other—to have you approach a biblical text in bite-sized steps, and only then to have you contact other sources. Taking these out of order will destroy the "conversational partnership" among the participants, essentially moving the text further away from you—like talking to someone from across a crowded room. Keep the sessions in order.

3. Can Be Used on Your Own or in a Group

You can use PROBE on your own, as described above. Or you might choose a group setting, where it works especially well. Using the *PROBE Template Guides* for each day (see Appendix A), all participants would have daily readings during the week. Then in the group, you would all talk about the text you have been jointly reading, and you would share (1) experiences and outcomes, (2) the questions you asked and still have, (3) the steps you took, (4) the solutions you reached, and most of all (5) how to apply this text to your life now.

    a. The group leader might come up with questions to address during the daily readings.

    b. Or, each person in the group might be asked to come up with their two biggest questions from this text.

    c. Or, to start out, you might like some prewritten material made specifically for this purpose.[99] This way, you could learn the process through guided lessons.

---

[99] See the *Unrelenting Faith* material at the very end of this book.

A Principle

There is a main and guiding principle at work here: *Always do your own work first* (**P-R-O** B-E) *before you let anyone else tell you what a block of text is about (which happens at* P-R-O **B**-E). You'll read one block of text (usually from 1 to 20 verses or so, or maybe a whole chapter). You'll do this all week long, over and over again in different translations. If you get impatient or in a hurry, wanting to keep on reading, you will subvert the process. Finally, you will *engage the author (E)*. If you treat this like a conversation with someone you really want to talk to, your experience will be enhanced.

This is a *process*. Reading the Bible through in a year is fine thing, but this is not that. This slows the pace, to get more intentional; and it fastens the gaze, to allow for more insight, comprehension, and interaction. This approach juxtaposes two poles:

Repetition ⟷ **Daily Variety**

When used together, these create an effective approach to Bible engagement that is also deeply satisfying.

A Pronouncement

There is **one big rule**: *Do not allow yourself to read from any other source during* **P-R-O** B-E—*except for English Bible translations!* It is also good to have a concordance for day P-R **O**-B-E (Observe). You'll need it. A concordance is a primary study tool that helps you look at words within texts. Translations and a concordance are *primary* tools; all the rest (like commentaries, study Bible notes, and even talking to your Pastor) are all *secondary* tools. Use Bible software the same way. Don't let the software do all of your work for you—despite the fact that software companies actually come out and say theirs will! Software is very valuable, if kept in its place and used in the proper way and at the proper times.[100]

You want to get in the habit of always reading the biblical text first before you let others tell you what it means. The biggest mistake made by Bible readers across the board is that they are too quick to look up somebody else's answers or to grab a study Bible or commentary (or worse, just draw a quick opinion), before they have spent any time at all in the biblical text on their own.

The PROBE approach is a direct way of helping you to stop making quick opinions or too quickly moving into a "commentary" mentality. It moves all of this to a more proper time and occasion, *after you have already shaken hands with the text itself and started the conversation on your own.* It also helps you to stay focused on one text at a time without bouncing around all over the place.

Objections and Beyond

This approach directly says: *"If you really want more from the Bible then **get serious** about engaging it in conversation!"*

It is true that some people raise objections. "I've never done it this way." "I don't have time." "I don't like the approach." "I think using imagination is silly or dangerous." "This is not approved by my pastor." "I don't get it—it's too hard." "I don't like to write!" "It is not how I learn." Such objections are true for the people who raise them. Not everyone wants to learn a new skill. We are all different people.

But others have quite a different experience. Those who approach with energy for learning a new skill and who commit themselves to the process have amazing things happen for them. For example, this new conversational emphasis has transformed

---

[100] If you don't know what some of these tools are (like Bible dictionaries or concordances, or how to use them), that would be what more study would bring. It is not the purpose of this book to teach about all of the potential tools or how to use them. You could, however, check out *BibleDashboard.com* for a lot more on such things. Especially look at the area "Word Study Helps."

not only my relationship with biblical texts, but with God and with my fellow believers. Others have similar experiences and enjoy living with its value. It is an energetic approach to biblical texts that puts us in conversation with their various authors—a step-by-step way of starting and sustaining that conversation.

This, then, is PROBE Basic. We have seen a simple but powerful process that can easily fit a 5-day schedule. But what if we want even more. What then?

We arrive, now, at our denouement—the cherry on top: PROBE Prime.

_13_

PROBE
Prime

What if you want an even deeper conversation with a biblical author than you can get with PROBE Basic? What if you have a bigger Bible study project or interest? What do you do then?

The answer to this might surprise you.

You CAN'T Outgrow It

First, *PROBE Basic helps you learn the ropes and is often all you need.* This is, in fact, what I myself follow. If I need more flexibility or time, I simply move into PROBE Prime. (I'll get to that below.)

Second, *you can't outgrow this approach—it's scalable!* A light needs to go on here. Scalability is everything: you are learning a process, a specific order in which to proceed. Once you learn that process in PROBE Basic, you can apply it to any biblical text of any size (even whole books) or to any study project of any depth. You will simply automatically slide seamlessly over to PROBE Prime.

Such a flexible and scalable approach makes possible an overarching organizational structure into which any other method or combination of methods will fit, and it keeps you on track for what big steps need to be taken, and when. So, once you get a little experience with the 5-step layered process of PROBE Basic, you will carry a picture of *the conversation path* in your head, no matter how small or large the project is. It will scale to the size you need.

In fact, here is what will fit into the PROBE structure:

1. simple or light conversations;
2. all devotional or contemplative approaches;
3. all of the most technical and academic biblical study disciplines[101]

PROBE does not compete with or replace existing methods, because it is not (technically speaking) a method. It is rather an *organizing structure—a path*—that allows already existing methods to plug-in and do their work at the proper time.

Such methods (listed only generally above) don't come into effect until at least day P-R-**O**-B-E (Observe) or maybe even day B (for Brainstorm). The reason is, all study methods are specific tools for finding specific things. And they never—*never!*—supplant the need, first and foremost, to spend time in the biblical text *yourself*, holding off what others have to say until an appropriate time.

As an example, if you are wanting to approach a biblical text devotionally, you would still *read the biblical text first*. Do **P-R-O-B-E** as laid out. You might do these over three days, or you might

---

[101] All will fit right inside this approach (even though some might object that they don't fit there). I am actually a big fan of a wide variety of academic study disciplines, including historical critical methods (there are many) and also literary critical methods (just as many or more), and even more specifically oriented approaches. They are all designed to look for specific things; they are like specific tools in a carpenter's tool shed. The problem is, far too often, the people using these tools act like they have the *only tool in the shed*, when they might not even have the *sharpest* tool. No one who is not an academic needs to worry about learning or using such tools—they are for specialists who often use them to great benefit, even though these methods are often highly debated even among those specialists. In our own study, such people and methods can (might) be accessed during O and B (sessions 3 and 4) to see what they might add. But nobody anywhere can cover everything, and that is never the point of any of this. The point here is that whether they like it or not, they fit in this schedule at a particular place, and that is the only place they fit!

do them one right after the other, even during the same session. The P-R-**O**-B-E (Observe) stage might be quite light, but you still try to recap the gist of the text and you still look for key words and maybe ask a few questions to the author. If you have additional devotional material, you would still not bring it in until stage P-R-O-**B**-E (Brainstorm). In other words, you don't simply start out by reading the devotional material. *You always read the biblical text first!* You always try to see its author first, and shake hands!

This approach will certainly help and guide beginners. But this approach will scale as far as you want to go with it (see next chapter).

You CAN Water it Down—Don't!

Although I have said this earlier in the book (especially chapters 3 and 4, *Spirit* and *Text*), I need to repeat it here: *don't water this down!* If you do, you will actually be throwing cold water on the texts themselves.

It might be a wonderful experience to sit by the lake, read a biblical text, pray, and feel uplifted. I'm not decrying that; but that is *not* what I mean by having a conversation with a biblical author. Such a lake-side experience may be a conversation of sorts, but it is more often a conversation with myself as I use a biblical text to reflect on myself. However much I might like that, I am not talking about just sitting with a text and calling it "conversation." I'm talking about specific moves *to actually respect what the authors are **trying** to do* by listening to and interacting with them through their texts. That is a completely different thing.

What Makes it Prime!

This is completely scalable. For larger projects, you can simply ignore the "day" limitations and the O and B sessions over weeks or even months. I do this routinely when I'm working on major study projects.

To illustrate, here's a sample of the PROBE process on a bit of a deeper quest. If you are a beginner, you might feel overwhelmed by what I'm about to say. But you should read it all the more eagerly to see what is possible if you start getting really hungry for more.

It starts on day 1, but then it proceeds without reference to any "days." I am describing my own process as I am pursuing a conversation with Paul over an unnamed block of text. This could be any text block.

PR: <u>Pre-Read and Recap</u>: You will notice that I have joined P and R, starting them together; and I am no longer concerned about how long things take.

1. After a good deal of prayer, I'll *read* the text by translating it from Greek.[102] I'll write out my translation, and keep it handy as a working text. This might take me an hour or days, it depends on the text. I spend whatever time I need to do it.

2. So far, I'm primarily just reading, not trying to do anything fancy. I want to *shake hands* with this text and with its author. To do that, I translate it and then I recap (i.e., I summarize *in writing*) what I think is going on in this text. I always make the recap shorter than the text.

3. Now I have welcomed this author into my room. I don't go read anything about this author from anybody right now. I don't care what they think, yet. I want to simply meet this author.

O <u>Observe</u>: Now I start looking closely at the text *observing* it often word by word. *This is the time and place the real conversation begins.*

1. I pick out what appear to be key or difficult words or phrases. I'll use my computer software concordance programs or

---

[102] Obviously, most people cannot do this! Not beginners and not most advanced Bible readers! That is fine! You would start with your own Bible and other English translations. You would never need to go past those. But for those interested in even more, we solve this problem too! See Collier 2019.

even my hard copy Greek and English concordances to do word studies and phrase searches.[103]

2. I will look for, and I will certainly and eagerly, look up any *echoes, allusions, or quotations* of other authors this text might be making.[104] I will also *always, always, always* pay attention to the contexts from which those things come. Even though this could actually—all by itself—add days, weeks or months to my time here, *that is why I'm here! This is not a side note!* This can open many incredible doors for how this author is *thinking with* and *conversing with* others. And they might not be exactly the same! This now becomes a focus for me.

3. I might spend days, weeks, or on really big projects, even months on this step (**Observe**): I want to know what is going on in this text! I don't mind long and detailed conversations: that is when we get to know each other!

4. From start to finish in this **Observe** process, I am talking to the author in the chair behind me. (In my own physical setup, the biblical author sits behind me in a chair higher than mine, always looking over my shoulder. Obviously you don't have to do it this way.) I might even find myself blurting out loud things like, "Paul, what in the world are you doing here? Why did you put this word here, why this phrase! Why are these words put in this order?" When I do that, I know that Paul will start to answer my questions *from the text.*

5. I might also start to apply certain *advanced study methods* during this step, if they are needed or appropriate, but I won't go into those because they are highly technical. The point is, they would fit here.

---

[103] *Accordance, Logos* or some other Bible program. Beginners can start with *Strong's* or *Young's Concordance* or a newer one, but they should hope to graduate from these older and less versatile sources as they are able. They can be useful, just like a horse and buggy can still be faster than walking. But it is better to get some good Bible software for your computer, tablet, or phone. You only need one.

[104] This is not the same as "running center column references." This is looking for intentional quotations or allusions to OT texts by my author. E.g., 1Cor 10:7 intentionally and directly quotes Ex 32:6. Just running center column references should NOT be done until step 4. The goal now is to see what *this* author is doing.

6. This is key: *The kinds and quality of the questions I ask and seek are crucial.* If I ask questions not really related to the text, I will end up simply making up answers out of thin air. That is not what we want to do. We want to listen to the text! If we ask text-related questions, these will drive us back into the text to search for answers. We don't just make up answers based on what we want to hear at that moment.

B: **Brainstorm**: Now that I'm familiar with this text and think I have some idea of what is going on with it myself, I invite others to my table—*I want to make this a broader conversation.*

1. At this point,[105] I'll bring in as many English translations,[106] books, journal articles, Bible dictionaries, encyclopedias, a good Bible atlas, commentaries, and other studies of various kinds, as I can get my hands on[107]—I might even write or call two or three people I trust and talk to them about it.

2. I want to know what all of these "conversation partners" of mine (books or people) see in this text. What are they *missing*? What did *I* miss?

3. It is an arrogant thing to think that we don't need conversation with others who have spent their lives on such questions. But we don't *ever* do this until we do our own work in this text first!

E: **Engage**. Finally, and ultimately, I want to engage the author about this text I have just spent so much time with. I will usually start writing! Once in a while, I'll turn my chair around and speak to the author in the chair behind me, the one who has been looking over my shoulder all of this time—as if a friend and I are working on something together. But usually, I do this step by writing. I'll start organizing my notes, summing things up, and drawing some conclusions. ***This conversation is not over till I do this!***

---

[105] This is another part that will overwhelm beginners. You don't *start* like this. You start out, here, by simply finding another source or two to broaden your conversation.

[106] Obviously, English readers are using these from day 1. There is no obligation ever to go beyond them—unless you are truly hungry for more.

[107] You can find recommendations I've made here: BibleDashboard.com, look under Special Tools.

1. I certainly pray about it.

2. I might go through the checklist of questions for step 5; but (more likely) I might just start organizing and writing. It depends on the text and what I found.

3. I rarely ever write on paper; I usually type everything on my computer. By now I have a whole computer folder full of sub-folders and files with all my notes.

4. When I'm done, I might publish what I've been working on—in a blog post, or to my study partners, or even in an article or book. Like this one.

The conversation is now over, at least for the moment. However, like all other conversations, it is now part of me. It now forms the backdrop for all other conversations I will ever have with this biblical author or any other.

Minds Trained by Practice

Before bringing this book to a close, I want to talk about the utter significance of what we are seeking as fellow students of the Bible. For what we are talking about is specifically modeled in Heb 5:14:

*Solid food is for adults with minds **trained by practice** to distinguish between good and bad. (NJB)*

If you are a Bible reader—whether a beginner or someone who has been reading for quite a long time—and if you think to yourself, "Yes, I'm serious about getting more from the Bible!" your attention should be *riveted* to this right now! *Minds trained by practice* is a fine translation, but look closer. It kind of looks like this in Greek, only now with English letters:

*tēn **hexin** ta aisthētēria **gegumnasmena***

Yes, it's Greek to me, too. But in Greek the word "practiced" is from **gumnazō** (the last word), and from this we get *gymnasium*. It literally meant *"to train and to undergo discipline."* Also, the

135

second word **hexin** literally meant "brought into current shape by doing something again and again."[108]

The picture you should hold in your head is *working out at the gym for the sake of cultivating discipline!*

Hebrews isn't done yet. It brings this whole concept of growth up again in 12:11 when the word *to train* is used specifically with another word for *discipline*:

> **Discipline!** *(paideia)*
> *It never seems like joy,*
> *just pain!*
> *It is only later,*
> *as a delightful end-result*
> *of those who through this* **discipline**
> **have been trained (i.e., have steadily "worked out"),**
> *that the payoff comes:*
> *You are [finally!] set right!*

Biblical Conversation holds great promise for those who want more out of their time in biblical texts.

Stop Reading the Bible!

Yes, stop! That's how we started; that is where we will end. Take its authors out for coffee instead. Learn how to engage them in conversation through their texts. There is a huge difference in the two approaches.

In Part 1, we took stock of the **opportunity** in front of us. By reviewing various *styles* of Bible reading, we exposed the inter-relationship of text and self. Here we identified a prime directive (an overriding, guiding mandate) when handling biblical texts:

---

[108] In Greek the phrase is τὴν ἕξιν τὰ αἰσθητήρια γεγυμνασμένα in Heb 5:14 BGT, "having worked out again and again one's capacity for discernment." The object here is the ability to distinguish good from evil so that we might make good choices. Anyone dealing with life knows that these choices show up every single day, both large and small. In the context of Hebrews 5-6, the emphasis is on growth beyond spiritual puberty. The word *gumnazō* also occurs 1Tim 4:7 "Train yourself to be like God"; and in 2Pet 2:14, don't be "trained in your own personal cravings."

*Our primary concern when handling biblical texts is to respect
what the authors of those texts are trying to do. All approaches
that call themselves "Bible Study" should seek to get in touch with
that, and then stay in touch with that.*

In Part 2 we took a few steps on an incredible **journey**. We
identified three different shades of biblical conversation. We
focused on Shade 3—*how biblical authors were in constant
conversation with each other.* This has stunning ramifications for
how we view the Bible as a collected book today, and for how we
view ourselves. Are we still in conversation with these ancient
authors, or do we spend more time reading as outsiders in some
kind of top-down reading model?

Part 3 was all about **metamorphosis—how we transform our
Bible reading lives.** We noted two actions:

The first was **preparation.** We set about to create a *mindset*, a
healthy *expectation*, and a *physical space.* This helps us make room
for conversation. One of the reasons Christians are so rampantly
illiterate about the Bible is that, generally speaking, we don't take
"our closet" (our private space)[109] as a crucial *place of preparation.*

The second was **conversation** itself—very specific, step-by-step
actions to take us directly into conversation with God through
biblical authors and their texts. The approach laid out is not a
heavy burden, hard to bear; nor is it grievous. It is, in fact,
surprisingly easy to learn and easy to model for others. Indeed, it
champions responsible, contextual, and conversational Bible
study, and it provides a specific means of achieving it.

The only question is, "Are we willing?"

Biblical Conversation holds great promise for those with a
ready heart—for those who understand that conversation with
God is the one and only hope of humanity.

---

[109] See chapter 11.

Appendix

P	R	O	B	E
Pre-Read	Recap	Observe	Brainstorm	Engage
Day 1	Day 2	Day 3	Day 4	Day 5

—A—
PROBE Template Guides

Here are 5 generic step-by-step starter templates, one for each letter: **P-R-O-B-E.** These are expanded versions of the 5-step process used by both PROBE Basic and PROBE Prime.

They can be used for any block of biblical text.[110]

It is important to *keep these in order,* whether you follow a daily plan or not. They build progressively towards a goal of a conversational cycle.

If you want a more specific take-you-by-the-hand guide, you should check out the *Unrelenting Faith* series in the back of this book. This series has a reader, a PROBE manual, and a leader's guide for small groups.[111]

---

[110] A "biblical text" or "block of text" would be any self-contained unit of a text, including a sentence, paragraph, chapter, Psalm, larger block, or whole book with which you have decided to interact. E.g., just one verse (1Th 1:5, even though in Greek, 5:2-10 is one long sentence); or the Lord's Prayer (Mt 6:9-15); or the Sermon on the Mount (Mt 5-7); or 1Corinthians 13; and Genesis 1, or 1-3; or Psalm 23; etc.

[111] *Unrelenting Faith* is a series built specifically around this PROBE process. It provides a conversational reader plus a PROBE Journal. It takes you by the hand and walks you step by step through the process as you get comfortable with it. See Appendix A for templates, and see Collier 2015b complete series of books.

P	R	O	B	E
Pre-Read	Recap	Observe	Brainstorm	Engage
Day 1	Day 2	Day 3	Day 4	Day 5

1. Pre-Read: This is a *hands free* day. No writing.

Begin by setting the stage. Just as you might prepare if someone were coming to your house, prepare for this conversation. Get a favorite drink and sit down across the table from this person, the author of our letter.

1. Remind yourself: **I-FACE the Text** (from ch9).
2. Pray about this time you're about to have.
3. **Read your text** from two different English translations.
4. Don't write anything. Don't mark anything. Don't look up anything. Let this text make an impression on you. Just soak it up.
5. Now spend time in prayer about that text and about your life. Don't be in a hurry, here. Take your time.

On this day, don't do anything more with this. Don't look up words, don't make notes. Your goal is simply to listen. Just as if you were sitting across the table with someone talking. This gives you time today to simply think about the text you're reading, and for patient prayer.

It is possible to combine steps 1 and 2, to allow more time with steps 3 or 4.

DO NOT read commentaries, study Bible notes, or other such things. Just make this about *listening to* today's text.

Make this your first step every time with each new text you read.

P	**R**	O	B	E
Pre-Read	Recap	Observe	Brainstorm	Engage
Day 1	**Day 2**	Day 3	Day 4	Day 5

2. Recap: Today is about *listening and recapping.*

Don't be asking, "What does this means for me?" That comes later.

Put yourself into *listening mode,* just like you want somebody to really listen to you. Put down your own questions. Today, listen to this text for its own sake so that you can say, "Here is what I think you are saying."

Have a notebook so you can start recording your notes.

1. Remind yourself: **I-FACE the Text** (from ch9).
2. Pray about this time in the text, that God will give you a heart seeking conversation.
3. **Read your text again** in any translation (preferably different from yesterday).
4. Using your notebook, write a note to the author of this piece. Don't get hung up with thoughts like, "but God is the real author!" Whatever else you think about this, at the very least, God chose a human author to write this. Speak to the human author right now. If you don't know who it is, it does not matter. Write to that unknown author.
5. Say something like this: "Paul (or whoever), here is what I hear you saying." Then recap exactly what you think is being said.
6. In your own words, summarize the main point(s) that the writer said to you.
7. Don't write a commentary. Make it shorter than the actual text.
8. Now pray about this, that God will help you consider these things all day.
9. That's all. You're done. Don't keep going. Let this sink-in during today.

DO NOT read commentaries, study Bible notes, or other such things. Just make this about you and today's text.

This is the second step. It is possible to combine this with step 1 on the first day to give you more time with steps 3 or 4.

P	R	O	B	E
Pre-Read	Recap	Observe	Brainstorm	Engage
Day 1	Day 2	**Day 3**	Day 4	Day 5

3. Observe: Today is about *looking closely* at your text.

Start asking: "What is going on in this text?" You still are in listening mode, but now much more actively.

Now you start turning this into a real conversation. For the past two days you've been listening. Show respect to the biblical text by paying it the same honor you want others to show you.

1. Remind yourself: **I-FACE the Text** (from ch9).
2. Pray about this time in the text, that God will give you energy and a heart for engagement.
3. **Read your text again**. This time, identify and circle (or write down) key words and ideas. Pay special attention to the flow of the argument.
4. Take notes in your notebook.
5. Now start asking the author questions.
   a. Especially "**why**" questions. "Why did you put that sentence there? Why did you say it like that? Why this word rather than another word?"
   b. Also "**what**" questions. "What does that word mean? That phrase? That concept?" (Ask him! Actually say things like, "Paul, why did you do this? What are you trying to do?" It)
   c. This is where you **start doing word studies.** Use a concordance and maybe a word dictionary (a lexicon, not a "Bible Dictionary"—that is a mini-encyclopedia) to learn how key words are used in other texts.
   d. Are there any direct quotations or allusions to OT texts? If so, look them up and start reading their contexts. This is not the same as looking up all the cross references that might be listed. Your goal is see if your text is *intentionally* quoting or alluding to an OT text.

It is possible to combine steps 1 and 2, to allow more time with steps 3 or 4.

You CAN use a concordance and dictionary (lexicon) today. However, STILL DO NOT read commentaries, study Bible notes, or other such things.

P	R	O	**B**	E
Pre-Read	Reason	Observe	**Brainstorm**	Engage
Day 1	Day 2	Day 3	**Day 4**	Day 5

4. Brainstorm: Today you *open up* the conversation.

Now you invite other conversation partners to the table.

So far, we've only had eyes for our biblical text, only listening to and interacting with the author himself. But now we invite others into the conversation. Today, with the author still at your table, invite other guests to join you at your table.

1. Remind yourself: **I-FACE the Text** (from ch9).
2. Always start and end with prayer!
3. Now invite **other writers of biblical texts** (you can still use a concordance here, as yesterday): Paul, Matthew, Luke, etc. OT and NT alike. DON'T CONFLATE THEM!! (Resist this temptation! Allow them to be however different they actually are. These authors do not all have to agree with each other any more than you do with me! Cf., Paul with Peter!)
4. Next, invite translators and **scholars of all types** (commentaries, Bible dictionaries and encyclopedias, study Bibles, more).
5. Also invite **others** like your preacher, or some of your real-life trusted friends. You do this by writing them an email or calling with a question.

NOW allow yourself to read commentaries, study Bible notes, and other such things. Get into it!

Discuss this text with all of them. You *DO* want to listen to what they say. So here is the process: you will read, take notes, do word studies, etc. But *don't just sit there, talk back!* You've got things to add, too, based on the work you've already done. *Engage them all!*

Obviously, you have to say "when." This step can last for hours, days, weeks, or even years!

It is possible to combine steps 1 and 2, to allow more time with steps 3 or 4.

145

P	R	O	B	**E**
Pre-Read	Recap	Observe	Brainstorm	Engage
Day 1	Day 2	Day 3	Day 4	**Day 5**

5. Engage: Today is about *looking closely* at your text.

This is where you ask "So what?" and make applications.

Naturally, some of this has already happened and there is no nice and neat separation between all of these steps. But today we **focus** on applying this text to where we live. This is *bringing the word to life*.

There are several kinds of questions you can ask here that will help you engage the author. It helps to write your responses in your notebook.

1. Imagining Paul at your table, tell him what you learned this week from this text, e.g., what meant the most to you,

2. If you could ask Paul one question from this week, what would it be?

3. Thinking about what you've read this week, what kind of power can it bring to your own life?

    a. It has the power to help you *think or decide* what?

    b. It has the power to help you *do* what?

4. If Paul were writing this text directly to you or to your church, what specific point do you think he would want to make now?

5. Write at least one thing you can do today that will put this text into practice in your life.

6. Name at least one person you can "touch" within the next 3 days with some aspect of this text. And how will you do it?

7. Other notes or thoughts.

You are now finished with this conversation cycle. Take a couple of days off and start next week on a new one!

—B—
Definition & Features

Biblical Conversation is an act, but also an art. Understood and implemented responsibly, it can transform the way the Bible gets read and applied. Conversation can occur from two points of view: (1) how *they* (biblical authors) were engaging each other, and (2) how *we* might join in with them.

1. General Definition

Biblical Conversation is not, strictly speaking, a method. It is a means by which other disciplines are brought together and utilized for a single purpose. For the sake of clarity, here is a succinct, working definition.

> **Biblical Conversation** *is an artful encounter with biblical texts that treats them, not as mere* **objects** *to be read, but as living* **conversation partners** *to be engaged.*

2. Features

As an *artful* encounter, attention is given to *intuitive* listening to texts as well as *imaginative* engagement with them, in the same manner as with a friend over coffee. This kind of reading can be described as having several characteristics or features at once:

(1) *It is holistic:* It pulls from all the common disciplines in chapters 2-5. This is not a substitute for, but a way of utilizing the various disciplines together as needed. As holistic medicine treats the mind and spirit along with the body and sees them as inseparable parts of a whole, so *Biblical Conversation* welcomes the wide variety of available methods (both for text and self) when reading biblical texts. As in all good communication, the spotlight is on lively interactions with the texts as they appear in the context of the whole. This avoids ending up with segmented (or even cherry-picked) readings.

(2) *It is biblically timeless:* It recognizes that the inter-biblical conversations taking place among authors are not simply *historical* (as if, "Hey, look what they did back then!"). Instead, these are ongoing discussions that are still calling out for engagement. Even though these authors (some of whom we don't know) are all long-dead, they are still alive in their texts, and they are still speaking (Heb 11:4). Even then they were busy answering the question, "How do we deal with this now?" This is the basis for all efforts at *Biblical Conversation*. It is not about mimicking cultural methods; or digging up laws

(or letters) set in stone; it is about learning to think and converse theologically about ongoing concerns.

(3) *It is highly personal:* As with any personal conversation, a concern for logic, reason, and fairness is clearly legitimate. Even so, this is not some heady experiment. Meaningful conversation always includes intuition and imagination. For that reason, *Biblical Conversation* warmly encourages the development and use of intuitive and imaginative skills.

(4) *It points to God:* It aims to put every participant in search of a conversation with God—"face to face, like one might speak with a close friend" (Ex 33:11). This is not about satisfying a church or organizational requirement, like a faith or membership statement. This is concerned centrally about relationship with God.

(5) *It is replicatable[112]:* It is easy to replicate and to pass on to others. The biggest difficulty is getting past the unhealthy prejudices of previous reading habits. This approach can be explained in a way that provides a clear, easy, step-by-step, daily path for interacting with texts on both a responsible and highly personal basis. It can be taught, and it can be learned!

All of these features render *Conversational Bible Reading and Study* as an artful approach that respects both text and self in the pursuit of God.

---

[112] Purists prefer the spelling *replicable*. I'm not a purist. I think the longer spelling makes it more replicable among readers who are unfamiliar with it.

—C—
Resources Quoted

Primary Reference Works

Aland 1995   Aland, Kurt. *The Text of the New Testament an Introduction to the Critical Editions and to the Theory and Practice of Modern Textual Criticism.* 2nd rev ed. Eerdmans, 1995.

BDAG   W. Bauer, W. F. Arndt, F. W. Gingrich, and F. W. Danker, *A Greek-English Lexicon of the New Testament and Other Early Christian Literature.* 3rd edition. Chicago, 2000.

BDB   F. Brown, S. R. Driver, and C. A. Briggs, *Hebrew and English Lexicon of the Old Testament,* Oxford, 1907.

BDF   F. Blass, A. Debrunner, and R. W. Funk, *A Greek Grammar of the New Testament and Other Early Christian Literature.* Chicago, 1961.

BHS   K. Elliger and W. Rudolph, eds. *Biblia Hebraica Stuttgartensia.* Stuttgart: Deutsche Bibelgesellschaft, 1977).

Friberg   Friberg, Barbara; Friberg, Timothy; Miller, Neva F. *Analytical Lexicon Of The Greek New Testament.* Baker's Greek New Testament Library. Baker, 2000.

LXX   Alfred Rahlfs, ed. *Septuaginta,* Deutsche Bibelgesellschaft Stuttgart, 1979Septuagint.

NA28   Eberhard Nestle and Aland, Kurt, eds. *Novum Testamentum Graece,* 28th ed. Stuttgart: Deutsche Bibelgesellschaft, 2013.

UBS5   Eberhard Nestle and Aland, Kurt, eds. *UBS 5th Revised Greek New Testament.* German Bible Society, 2014.

Secondary Resources

Baker 2020   Baker, Ellen K. "Tending to Our Self" in *Caring for ourselves: A therapist's guide to personal and professional well-being,* (pp. 37-58). Washington, DC, US· American Psychological Association, 2003. Online at: https://psycnet.apa.org/buy/2003-04004-003

Brueggemann 2000   Brueggemann, Walter. *Spirituality of the Psalms.* Fortress, 2002.

Childs 1974   Childs, B. S. *Book of Exodus* OTL. Westminster John Knox, 1974.

Collier   See heading below: Publications by Gary D. Collier.

Diez Macho 1960   Diez Macho, A. "The Recently Discovered Palestinian Targum: Its Antiquity and Its Relationship to the Other Targums." *VTSup* VII (Congress Volume 1959). Leiden, 1960, 222-245.

Driver 1911   Driver, S. R. *Book of Exodus* CBSC (1911) 154-58.

Resources Quoted

Fay 2013   Greg Fay. *Inkblotitis: Christianity's Dangerous Disease. Book 1: The Disintegration of the Bible; Book 2. Rediscovering the Books of God.* Create Space, 2013.

Fee 2014   Fee, Gordon D. *How to Read the Bible for All Its Worth.* 4th ed. Zondervan, 2014.

Figal 2002   Figal, Günter "The Doing of the Thing Itself: Gadamer's Hermeneutic Ontology of Language." Translated by Dostal, Robert. In *The Cambridge Companion to Gadamer.* Cambridge, 2002.

Fishbane 1989 Fishbane, Michael. *The Garments of Torah: Essays in Biblical Hermeneutics.* IUPress, 1989.

Frascheri 1846 Frascheri, Giuseppe (1809-1886). "Paolo and Francesca in conversation with Dante and Virgil." Episode from Divine Comedy, by Dante Alighieri (1265-1321). Oil on canvas, Italy, 1846. http://www.gettyimages.com/detail/illustration/paolo-and-francesca-in-conversation-with-dante-and-stock-graphic/162275538

Gadamer 1960/2004 Gadamer, Hans-Georg. *Truth and Method.* 2nd rev. edition. Trans. J. Weinsheimer and D. G. Marshall. Originally published 1960. Bloomsbury Academic; 2 Revised edition, 2004.

Garland 2003 Garland, David E. *1Corinthians.* BECNT. Baker Academic, 2003.

Gray 1903   Gray, G. B. *Numbers* ICC, 1903.

Hagner 2006 Hagner, Donald A. "The Place of Exegesis in the Postmodern World." *History and Exegesis: New Testament Essays in Honor of Dr. E. Earle Ellis on His Eightieth Birthday.* Edited by Sang-won Son, S. Aaron Son. Bloomsbury T&T Clark, 2006.

Hays 1989   Hays, Richard B. *Echoes of Scripture in the Letters of Paul.* Yale, 1989.

Hays 1993   Hays, Richard B. "On the Rebound: A Response to Critiques of Echoes of Scripture in the Letters of Paul," in *Paul and the Scriptures of Israel,* edited by Craig A. Evans and James A. Sanders. JSNTSup, 83. SSEJC 1; Sheffield: JSOT, 1993, 70-97.

Hays 2005a Hays, Richard B. *The Conversion of the Imagination: Paul as Interpreter of Israel's Scripture.* Eerdmans, 2005.

Hays 2005b Hays, Richard B. "Who Has Believed Our Message? Paul's Reading of Isaiah." (Originally written in 1998.) *The Conversion of the Imagination: Paul as Interpreter of Israel's Scripture.* Eerdmans, 2005.

Hays 2009   Hays, Richard B., Stefan Alkier, Leroy A. Huizenga eds. *Reading the Bible Intertextually.* Baylor, 2009.

Hays 2013   Hays, Christopher M., and Ansberry, Christopher B. (eds). *Evangelical Faith and the Challenge of Historical Criticism.* SPCK, 2013.

Hays 2014   Hays, Richard B. *Reading Backwards: Figural Christology and Fourfold Gospel Witness.* SPCK 2014.

Hays 2016a Hays, Richard. *Echoes of Scripture in the Gospels.* Baylor, 2016.

Hays 2016b Hays, Richard B. "The Deep and Subtle Unity of the Bible." A conversation with Richard B. Hays. Interview by Garrett Brown, November/December 2016.

Resources Quoted

http://www.booksandculture.com/articles/2016/novdec/deep-and-subtle-unity-of-bible.html

Heinemann 1971   Heinemann, Joseph. "The Proem in the Aggadic Midrashim: A Form Critical Study." *Studies in Aggadah and Folk-Literature*, vol. 22. *Scripta Hierosolymitana*. Jerusalem: The Magnes, 1971.

Higginbottom 2020   Higginbottom, Twila. Private email, Friday, June 19, 2020 12:07 PM.

Hyatt 1971   Hyatt, J. P. *Exodus* NCBC, 1971.

Jacobson 1996   Jacobson, Howard. *A Commentary on Pseudo-Philo's Liber Antiquitatum Biblicarum, With Latin Text and English Translation.* Brill, 1996.

Johnson 2018   Johnson, John A. "The Psychology of Expectations: Why unrealistic expectations are premeditated resentments." *Psychology Today*, Posted Feb 17, 2018. Accessed July 12, 2020. https://www.psychologytoday.com/us/blog/cui-bono/201802/the-psychology-expectations

Keil 1869   Keil, C. F. and Delitzsch F. *Commentary on the Old Testament in Ten Volumes.* Vol 3, 1869. Reprint: 25 vols in 10. Eerdmans, 1982.

Klein 2017   Klein, William W., Blomberg, Craig L., Hubbard, Robert L. Jr. *Introduction to Biblical Interpretation.* 3rd ed. Zondervan, 2017.

Malherbe 2000   Malherbe, Abraham. *Letters to the Thessalonians.* AB 32B. Doubleday, 2000.

McKnight 2018   McKnight, Scot. *The Blue Parakeet: Rethinking How You Read the Bible.* 2nd ed. Zondervan, 2018.

Moule 1981   Moule, C. F. D., *The Birth of the New Testament.* BNTC. London: Adam and Charles Black, 1962. 3rd ed. 1981.

Noth 1962   Noth, M. *Exodus* OTL. SCM, 1962.

Noth 1968   Noth, M. *Numbers* OTL. John Knox, 1968.

Oestreich 2016   Oestreich, Bernhard. *Performance Criticism of the Pauline Letters.* Translated by Lindsay Ellias and Brent Blum. Biblical Performance Criticism 14. Cascade, 2016.

Porter 2006   Porter, Stanley ed. *Hearing the Old Testament in the New Testament.* Eerdmans, 2006

Sanders 1972   Sanders, James A. *Torah and Canon.* Fortress, 1972.

Sanders 1975/2001   Sanders, James A. "From Isaiah 61 to Luke 4." *Luke and Scripture: The Function of Sacred Tradition in Luke-Acts,* edited by Craig A. Evans and James A. Sanders, pp. 46-69. Originally published 1975. Wipf & Stock, 2001.

Sanders 1987   Sanders, James A. *From Sacred Story to Sacred Text: Canon as Paradigm.* Fortress, 1987.

Sanders 1993   Sanders, James A. "Paul and Theological History," in *Paul and the Scriptures of Israel,* edited by Craig A. Evans and James A. Sanders. JSNTSup, 83. SSEJC 1; Sheffield: JSOT, 1993, 52-57.

Wenham 1981   Wenham, G. J. *Numbers* TOTC. IVP, 1981.

Wright 1965   Wright, A. G. "The Structure of Wisdom 11-19" *CBQ* 27(1965): 28-34.

Publications by Gary D. Collier

Collier 1980	Collier, Gary D. Review of James G. D. Dunn. "Unity and Diversity in the New Testament," in *ResQ* 23:2 (1980): 121-126.
Collier 1983	Collier, Gary D. "The Problem of Deuteronomy: In Search of a Perspective." *ResQ* 26:4 (1983): 215-33.
Collier 1990	Collier, Gary D. "Bringing the Word to Life: Biblical Hermeneutics in Churches of Christ." *CS* 11:1 (October, 1990): 18-40.
Collier 1993	Collier, Gary D. *The Forgotten Treasure: Reading the Bible Like Jesus.* Howard Publishers, 1993.
Collier 1994	Collier, Gary D. "'That We Might not Crave Evil:' the Structure and Argument of 1Cor 10:1-13" *JSNT* 55 (1994) 55-75.
Collier 1995	Collier, Gary D. "Rethinking Jesus on Divorce." *ResQ* 37:2 (1995) 80-96.
Collier 2003	Collier, Gary D. *Divorce and the Christ-Community: A New Portrait.* CWP 2003.
Collier 2012	Collier, Gary D. *Scripture, Canon, & Inspiration: Faith in Pursuit of Conversation.* CWP, 2012.
Collier 2012a	Collier, Gary D. Review of James P. Ware (ed), *Synopsis of the Pauline Letters in Greek and English* (Baker Academic, 2010) for *SCJ* 15 no. 1 (2012): 150-152.
Collier 2015a	Collier, Gary D. ed., with Brian Casey. *Engaging Paul in 1Corinthians: A Celebratory Volume in Honor of John and Diana Eoff.* The Dialogē Press, 2015.
Collier 2015b	Collier, Gary D. *Unrelenting Faith. Volume 1: The Divine Secret.* Vol 2: *Rising above Struggle, Walking in Hope.* 1Thessalonians, Conversations 1-20. CCAP. The *Dialogē* Press, 2015 (with Journal).
Collier 2015c	Collier, Gary D. Review of Andrew E. Arterbury, W. H. Bellinger Jr., and Derek S. Dodson. *Engaging the Christian Scriptures: An Introduction to the Bible.* Baker, 2014 in *SCJ* 18 no. 2 (2015): 287-88.
Collier 2015d	Collier, Gary D. Review of Bruce W. Longenecker and Todd D. Still. *Thinking Through Paul: A Survey of His Life, Letters, and Theology.* Zondervan, in *SCJ* 18 no. 2 (2015): 313-315.
Collier 2016	Collier, Gary D. *Unrelenting Faith. Volumes 1&2: Conversations over Coffee with the Apostle Paul.* CWP. 2nd Edition, April 7, 2016.
Collier 2018	Collier, Gary D. *Graphē in Biblical and Related Literature.* Dialogē Press, 2018.
Collier 2019	Collier, Gary D. *Scribes Trained for the Kingdom. A Pre-Grammar for New Testament Greek as a Spiritual Discipline.* Dialogē Press, 2019.
Collier 2020	Collier, Gary D. *I Paulos. Shades of Conversation in 1Thessalonians. An Odyssey of Authors and Texts, and of Reading Paul Conversationally.* Dialogē Press, January 2017 (1st edition); July 2020 (Corrected ed. 4).

—D—
Abbreviations

For Ancient Works

BIBLICAL DOCUMENTS

All periods are omitted; Spaces are omitted in book names with numbers:
1Kgs not 1 Kgs; also 1Kings not 1 Kings.

Gen	1, 2Chr	Isa	Hos	Mt		
Ex	Ezra	Jer	Joel	Mk		
Lev	Neh	Lam	Amos	Lk		
Num	Esth	Ezek	Obad	Jn		
Deut		Dan	Jonah	Ac		
	Job		Mic			
Josh	Ps (Pss)		Nah	Rom	Heb	
Judg	Prov		Hab	1,2Cor	Jas	
Ruth	Eccl		Zeph	Gal	1, 2Pt	
	Song		Hag	Eph	1, 2, 3Jn	
1, 2Sam			Zech	Phil	Jude	
1, 2Kgs			Mal	Col	Rev	
				1, 2Th		
				1, 2Tim		
				Titus		
				Phlm		

OT APOCRYPHA

Wis	Wisdom of Solomon	Sir	Sirach (Ecclesiasticus)

PSEUDEPIGRAPHA

Ps-Philo	Pseudo-Philo *Biblical Antiquities*

PHILO OF ALEXANDRIA

Conf.	*De confusione linguarum*	*Legat.*	*Legatio ad Gaium*
Decal.	*De decalogo*	*Migr.*	*De migratione Abrahami*
Det.	*Quod deterius potiori insidari soleat*	*Mos. 1-2*	*De vita Mosis I, II*
Ebr.	*De ebrietate*	*Sacr.*	*De sacrificiis Abelis et Caini*
Leg. 1-3	*Legum allegoriae I, II, III*	*Somn. 1-2*	*De somniis I, II*

Rabbinic Texts

Midr. Tehillim	Midrash to the Psalms.
Num. R.	Numeri Rabbah (Midrash Rabbah to Numbers, B'midbar Rabbah).
Sukkah	A treatise in the Mishnah, Tosefta, and Babylonian Talmud

Targumic Texts

Tg. Neof.	*Targum Neofiti*	*Tg. Ps. -J.*	*Targum Pseudo-Jonathan*
Tg. Onq.	*Targum Onqelos*		

Josephus

Ant.	*Jewish Antiquities*

Greek & Roman Philosophy & Classics

Sen. Epistle Seneca, *Ad Lucilium Epistulae Morales*

English Translations of the Bible

English Translations from BibleWorks

ASV	American Standard Version (1901)
BBE	The Bible in Basic English (1949/64)
CEB	Common English Bible
CJB	Complete Jewish Bible
CSB	Holman Christian Standard Bible
CSB17	Holman Christian Standard Bible 2017
DBY	The Darby Bible (1884/1890)
DRA	The Douay-Rheims 1899 American Edition
ERV	English Revised Version (1885)
ESV	The English Standard Version (2007)
ETH	The Etheridge NT English Peshitta (1849)
GNV	Geneva (1599)
GWN	God's Word to the Nations Translation
HCSB	Holman Christian Standard Bible
JPS	Jewish Publication Society OT (1917)
KJA	King James (1611) Apocrypha
KJG	King James Version with Geneva Notes
KJV	King James (1611/1769) with Codes
LEW	The Lewis NT English Peshitta (1896)
LXA	LXX English Translation with Apocrypha (Brenton)

LXE	LXX English Translation (Brenton)
MGI	The Magiera NT English Peshitta (2006)
MIT	MacDonald Idiomatic Translation
MRD	The Murdock NT English Peshitta (1851)
NAB	The New American Bible
NAS	New American Standard Bible (1977) with Codes
NAU	New American Standard Bible (1995) with Codes
NET	The Net Bible
NIB	New International Version (UK 2011)
NIBO	New International Version (UK 1984)
NIrV	New International Readers Version
NIV	New International Version (1984) (US)
NJB	The New Jerusalem Bible
NKJ	New King James Version (1982)
NLT	New Living Translation
NOR	The Norton NT English Peshitta (1851)
NOY	GEORGE NOYES BIBLE (1869)
NRS	New Revised Standard Version (1989)
PNT	Bishops' New Testament (1595)
QBE	Dead Sea Scrolls Bible Biblical text
ROT	The Rotherham Bible (1999)
RPTE	Revised Patriarchal Greek Orthodox New Testament (2010)

Abbreviations

RSV	Revised Standard Version (1952)	GNT	Good News Translation
RWB	Revised Webster Update (1995) with Codes	ISV	International Standard Version
		JUB	Jubilee Bible
TNIV	Today's New International Version	KJ21	King James 21ˢᵗ Century
TNK	Jewish Publication Society Tanakh (1985)	LEB	the Lexham English Bible
		MSG	The Message
TNT	Tyndale New Testament (1534)	NCV	New Century Version
WEB	The Webster Bible (1833)	NEB	New English Bible
YLT	Young's Literal Translation (1862/1898)	NIRV	New International Readers Version
		NLV	New Life Version
		NMB	New Matthew Bible
English Translations		NTE	NT for Everyone
from Bible Gateway		OJB	Orthodox Jewish Bible
		PHL	and J. B. Phillips .
AMP	Amplified Bible	TLB	The Living Bible
CEV	Contemporary English Version	TPT	The Passion Translation
EHV	Evangelical Heritage Version	VOICE	The Voice
EXB	The Expanded Bible	WYC	Wycliffe Bible

Other Abbreviations

AB	Anchor Bible Commentary Series
BECNT	Baker Exegetical Commentary on the New Testament.
BNTC	Black's New Testament Commentaries
CBQ	*Catholic Biblical Quarterly*
CCAP	Conversations over Coffee with the Apostle Paul
CS	*Christian Studies*
CWP	Coffee With Paul
IABC	*Institute for the Art of Biblical Conversation*
IBR	*Institute for Biblical Research*
JSNT	*The Journal for the Study of the New Testament*
JSNTSup	Journal for the Study of the New Testament Supplement Series
JSOT	*Journal for the Study of the Old Testament*
MT	Masoretic Text (of the Hebrew Bible)
NCBC	New Century Bible Commentary
OTL	Old Testament Library
ResQ	*Restoration Quarterly*
SBL	Society of Biblical Literature
SCJ	*Stone-Campbell Journal*
SSEJC	Studies in Scripture in Early Judaism and Christianity
TOTC	Tyndale Old Testament Commentaries
VTSup	Vetus Testamentum Supplements
YHWH	Stands for the divine name of God: Yahweh or Jehovah

—E—
IABC Resources

The Unrelenting Faith Series
Designed specifically as an introduction to
a *Conversational* reading of the Bible

This study: 1Thessalonians

- 2 Readers (6 x 9, 164 pages)
- 2 Journals (8.5 x 11, 120 & 132 pages)
- 1 Leader's Guide (8.5 x 11, 82 pages)

A unique and engaging study series
for individuals, small groups, or whole churches.

- Volume 1: What Really Matters?
- Volume 2: Rising, Walking!
- Volume 3: Probe Journal 1
- Volume 4: Probe Journal 2
- Volume 5: Growing Groups (Leader's Guide)

For complete information on this new series go to this web page:

BiblicalConversation.com/uf/

Scripture, Canon, & Inspiration

Faith in Pursuit of Conversation

A new and challenging look at an old and perplexing topic.

"Collier has provided an engaging discussion of several critically important discussions going on among biblical scholars and leaders in churches today, namely, how did the Bible come to be and how should its inspiration be understood? He treats the subject matter seriously and fairly and is clear in his presentation. He is aware of the major issues related to his topics and presents them in a clear and convincing manner. While he will no doubt encounter opposition to several of his conclusions, he nevertheless makes reasonable arguments on the most important matters. I believe that those who read the Bible as the Word of God will gain many insights from this book. Collier wants his readers to consider carefully the issues he raises and those who do will gain a greater understanding of their Bible."

—**Lee Martin McDonald**, President Emeritus, Acadia Divinity College, Acadia University, Nova Scotia, Canada. A few recent books include: *The Origin of the Bible* (T&T Clark, 2011); *Non-canonical Religious Texts in Early Judaism and Early Christianity* (T&T Clark, 2012); and *The Formation of the Bible* (Hendrickson, 2012).

For complete information on this and other books go to:

BiblicalConversation.com/books/

Graphē in Biblical and Related Literature

Is the term *Scripture* an appropriate translation in English Bibles.

"This is as fine a discussion of the word "scripture" and its underlying Greek word, *graphē*, as you will find anywhere. This in-depth, historically oriented word study demonstrates how important a historical approach is to a correct understanding of the Bible.

While Dr. Collier's scholarship is of the highest quality, he is also a gifted teacher and communicator. His writing is clear and winsome. His book is filled with down-to-earth wisdom and he effectively debunks much nonsense spread by well-meaning, but poorly informed, Christians. Most importantly, he himself writes as a committed Christian with an earnest desire to advance the gospel in our needy world. I recommend this book with the greatest enthusiasm."

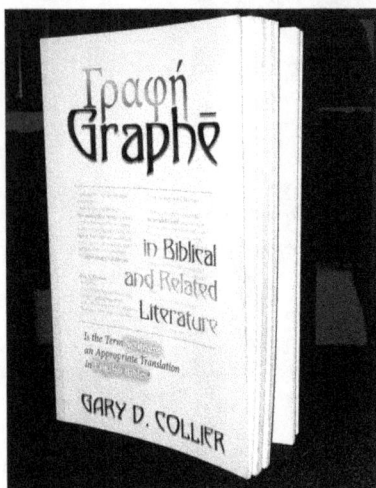

—**Donald A. Hagner**, Ph.D. George Eldon Ladd Professor Emeritus of New Testament Fuller Theological Seminary Pasadena, CA 91182. Among his recent works: *The New Testament: A Historical and Theological Introduction* (2012), and *How New is the New Testament? First-Century Judaism and the Emergence of Christianity* (2018) (Both from Baker Academic)

—F—
IABC

Institute for the Art of Biblical Conversation

Advanced Biblical Text Study
for those with uncommon interest in the biblical text

*Making a difference
for how people around the world
experience the Bible*

English Biblical Text

Greek Biblical Text:
Beginning and Advanced

Website:
BiblicalConversation.com

Contact Information:
Gary D. Collier
garydcollier@coffeewithpaul.com
Institute for the Art of *Biblical Conversation*
452 W Water St, Cloverdale, IN 46120

—G—
AUTHOR

Gary D. Collier
Ph.D., Biblical Studies,
Graduate Theological Foundation
in association with Oxford University

Director of *IABC*.
Author of several books on the interpretation of biblical texts.
BiblicalConversation.com/books

Teaches live, weekly, collaborative classes
based on English and Greek texts.

Complete author profile:
BiblicalConversation.com/gcollier.